Pace®

Family Recipe Round-Up

100 Easy Recipes from Pace Picante Sauce

TIME® LIFE BOOKS

Alexandria, Virginia

Campbell Soup Company

Camden, New Jersey

The PACE® Picante Sauce *Family Recipe Round-Up* 50th Anniversary Cookbook was produced by the Global Publishing division of Campbell Soup Company, Campbell Place, Camden, NJ 08103-1799.

Senior Managing Editor: Pat Teberg
Assistant Editors: Peg Romano, Ginny Gance
Marketing Manager: Linda Marshall
Director, Global Design Center: William Lunderman
Global Consumer Food Center: Sherry Hill, Debbie Conway, Patricia Ward, Joanne Fullan, Peggy Apice, Nancy Speth
Nutrition Science: Carole Dichter, D.Sc., R.D.; Patricia Locket, M.S., R.D.
Photography: Stephen Hone, Stephen Hone Studio/Philadelphia
Photo Stylists/Production: Clare Hone, Ruth Bowen, Jackie Neal, Tracy Coles, Jeannine Kearns
Food Stylists: Debbie Wahl, assisted by Berry Lauro, Nancy McClunin, Judy Stern

Pictured on the front cover: Chicken with Picante Black Bean Sauce (recipe page 55).

Preparation and Cooking Times: Every recipe was developed and tested in Campbell's Global Consumer Food Center by professional home economists. All recipes were tested with the medium variety of picante sauce. For families with children, mild and extra-mild varieties of picante sauce are available. Use "Chill Time," "Cook Time," "Marinating Time," "Prep Time" and "Stand Time" given with each recipe as guides. The preparation times are based upon the approximate amount of time required to assemble the recipes before baking or cooking. These times include preparation steps, such as chopping; mixing; cooking rice, pasta, vegetables; etc. The fact that some preparation steps can be done simultaneously or during cooking is taken into account. The cook times are based on the minimum amount of time required to cook, bake or broil the food in the recipes.

Recipe and Nutrition Values: Values are approximate; calculations are based upon food composition data in the Campbell Soup Company Master Data Base. Some variation in nutrition values may result from periodic product changes.

Calculation of Nutritional Information: Optional ingredients are omitted. When a choice is given for an ingredient, calculations are based on the first choice listed. Garnishes are not included in the calculations. The following information is provided for each recipe serving: calories, total fat, saturated fat; total carbohydrate, dietary fiber and protein in grams (g); and cholesterol and sodium in milligrams (mg).

For sending us glassware, flatware, dinnerware and serving accessories, a special thanks to: *Christofle,* New York, NY on pages 40, 67; *Dansk International Designs, Ltd.,* Mount Kisco, NY on the front cover and pages 31, 40, 45, 48, 75, 83, 109; *The Denby Pottery Company,* New York, NY on page 71; *Home Grown,* Manayunk, PA, pages 12, 36, 90; *Ikea,* Plymouth Meeting, PA on pages 24, 35, 60, 65, 67, 83, 87, 90, 98, 101, 105, 106; *The Little Nook,* Philadelphia, PA on pages 19, 31, 35, 105; *Mikasa,* Secaucus, NJ on pages 21, 28, 45, 60, 79, 83, 87, 89, 97, 106; *Nikko Ceramics Inc.,* Wayne, NJ on page 75; *Oneida Silversmiths,* Oneida, NY on pages 24, 33, 43, 55, 72, 95; *The Pfaltzgraff Co.,* York, PA on pages 21, 55, 64, 79, 102; *Sasaki,* New York, NY on the front cover and pages 16, 43, 71, 73, 76, 88, 94; *Susanna Hauser,* Philadelphia, PA on page 80; *Swid Powell,* New York, NY on page 19; *Tumbleweed,* Manayunk, PA on page 36.

Published by Time-Life Custom Publishing.
TIME-LIFE is a trademark of Time Warner Inc. U.S.A.

First printing. Printed in U.S.A.

Library of Congress Cataloging-in-Publication Data
PACE family recipe round-up/(Campbell Soup Company).
p. cm.
Includes index.
ISBN 0-7835-4861-3
1. Cookery (Hot pepper sauces)
2. Hot pepper sauces.
I. Campbell Soup Company.
TX819.H66P33 1996
641.8' 14—dc20

96-28262
CIP
Books produced by Time-Life Custom Publishing are available at special bulk discount for corporate and promotional use.
Call 1-800-323-5255.

Contents

Legend

Bold & Spicy

Contest Winner

Classic Recipe

30 Minutes or Less

Low Fat

It Takes A Legend To Make One

And David Pace qualifies as a sure-fire American legend.

He began his own business using rented space in the back of a liquor store in San Antonio, Texas. With the know-how gained from his family's syrup business, he cooked and bottled jellies and jams every morning and delivered them from the back of his truck in the afternoon. Along the way, David Pace began experimenting with a spicy blend of tomatoes, fresh jalapeño peppers and onions. His goal—to create the world's first fresh-tasting bottled Picante Sauce!

In 1947, it all came together. First there was the perfect recipe. Then the processing secret that kept the sauce fresh in the jar.

David Pace, 1963

4

Finally, there was the name—coined by David Pace—Picante Sauce. The rest is history.

Almost immediately, David Pace was selling all the sauce he could make throughout the region. He defied conventional wisdom by eliminating his 58 other products to focus solely on the marketing and production of his Picante Sauce. The original recipe had a medium heat level. In 1981, PACE introduced a hot and mild version. Then, in 1989, came the introduction of Thick & Chunky Salsa. Today, PACE is the number one Mexican sauce maker in the industry.

an and Cheese Quesadillas,
age 18

We like to say that David Pace led the Mexican Sauce revolution in America. His introduction of PACE Picante Sauce as an all-purpose condiment helped the market grow from nothing in 1947 to over 750 million dollars in annual sales today. With PACE products leading the way, Mexican sauces have overtaken ketchup as the nation's number one condiment. Now that's the stuff of legends and it sure is tasty.

On The Trail Of The Fresh Jalapeño

FRESH JALAPEÑOS in EVERY JAR

Right from the start, freshness set PACE Picante Sauce apart. And fresh flavor requires fresh ingredients—including fresh jalapeños, the little green peppers that give PACE its big bite. Now that may sound simple, but no other major Mexican sauce maker has figured out how to do it. Only Pace Foods has the commitment to fresh and taste the pepper know-how to make it happen.

1950, David Pace holding peppers with contract farmer Barney Hasselfield.

PACE never uses soggy "brined" jalapeños. Instead, they've accepted the challenge of keeping the processing plant supplied with fresh jalapeños year 'round. PACE's Pepper Experts have cultivated pepper farmers from California, Texas, Florida and Mexico. By following the jalapeño crop south, PACE ensures that its sauces are made from 100% fresh jalapeños day in, day out.

That commitment to freshness continues right to the grocery store shelves. Every jar of PACE sauce is "date-coded" and any jars over their date limits are removed from the shelves. This date coding helps ensure that every jar sold meets PACE's extraordinarily high fresh-taste standards.

In The Lab With Doctor "Pepper"

Dr. Lou Rasplicka in his kitchen laboratory

Lou Rasplicka, Ph.D. Food Science, is PACE's Vice-President of Technology and a world renowned authority on jalapeños. In fact, it is rumored he can tell where a pepper was grown and how much rainfall it received simply by tasting it. Not only does he know peppers, he develops new ones. It took four and a half years to breed PACE's special No-Heat jalapeño (patent pending), which is key to making PACE's extra-mild sauces flavorful without adding heat.

Pick Up The Pace ®!

It's more than a slogan; it's a way of doing business that adds up to red-hot success.

The success began when David Pace decided to market his new Picante Sauce as an all-purpose condiment—not simply a specialty sauce for Mexican foods. Every decision along the way was equally far sighted. Just consider the introduction of the hourglass-shaped jar. David Pace designed it to be attractive—so it could be put right on the table—as well as stable—so it wouldn't tip over. Today it's a registered trademark and a distinctive part of the PACE personality.

Another big breakthrough came in 1983 with the launch of the "Not From New York City" advertising campaign. It's based on the fact that PACE has the flavor born in San Antonio, Texas, "where folks know what salsa should taste like." The campaign is a series of uproarious cowboy spoofs emphasizing the fresh taste of PACE and its authentic origin.

The result of PACE's single-minded focus on its product and marketing is over-whelming success. Today Americans consume 120 million pounds of PACE sauces each year and PACE is the most popular Mexican sauce maker in the country. And with all that behind them, the company continues to forge ahead—always looking for new ways to Pick Up The PACE®!

With PACE's 50th anniversary cookbook, you can treat your friends and family to more than 100 delicious recipes and innovative menu ideas sprinkled throughout—you'll find these menus perfect for easy family suppers and casual entertaining. **Enjoy!**

In 1994, PACE's TV campaign reached such popularity that it was featured as a question on the TV game show Jeopardy. *The answer: "A Picante Sauce not made in New York City." The winning question: "What is PACE Picante Sauce?"*

Legend

Bold & Spicy

Contest Winner

Classic Recipe

30 Minutes or Less

Low Fat

Appetizers Hot & Cold

Chili con Queso Bites

PREP TIME: 10 MINUTES
COOK TIME: 10 MINUTES

4 eggs, beaten
1/2 cup PACE Picante Sauce
1/4 cup all-purpose flour
2 teaspoons chili powder
1 1/2 cups shredded Cheddar cheese (6 ounces)
1 green onion, chopped (about 2 tablespoons)

1. Preheat oven to 400°F. Grease 24 (3-inch) muffin-pan cups.
   Set aside.

2. In medium bowl mix eggs, picante sauce, flour and chili
   powder. Stir in cheese and onion.

3. Spoon about *1 tablespoon* cheese mixture into each cup.
   Bake 10 minutes or until golden brown. Serve warm or at
   room temperature with additional picante sauce.
   Makes 24 appetizers.

TIP: Baked appetizers may be frozen. To reheat, bake frozen
appetizers at 350°F. for 10 minutes or until hot.

*Pictured clockwise from top: Classic con Queso Dip (page 11), Hot 'n' Honeyed
Chicken Wings (page 16) and Chili con Queso Bites (page 11).*

Lightening Quick Snacks
Classic con Queso Dip
*Combine 1 pound cubed pasteurized
process cheese food and 1/2 cup PACE
Picante Sauce. Heat until cheese melts.
Serve with tortilla chips or fresh vegetables
for dipping.*

Classic Cream Cheese Spread
*Pour PACE Picante Sauce over 8 ounces
cream cheese, softened. Serve with crackers
and fresh vegetables.*

Quick and Easy Nachos
*Sprinkle shredded Cheddar cheese on
tortilla chips and bake. Top with
PACE Picante Sauce.*

PREP TIME: 25 MINUTES
COOK TIME: 20 MINUTES

1/4 cup PACE Picante Sauce
1/4 teaspoon ground cumin
1/3 cup chopped cooked ham
1/3 cup shredded Monterey Jack cheese
1 package (15 ounces) refrigerated pie crust dough

1. Mix picante sauce, cumin, ham and cheese.

2. On lightly floured surface, unfold *1* pie crust. Cut into 10 (3-inch) rounds. Top half of each round with *2 teaspoons* cheese mixture. Moisten edges of rounds with water. Fold over and press edges together. Seal edges with fork. Repeat with remaining pie crust and cheese mixture.

3. Bake at 400°F. for 20 minutes or until golden. Serve warm with additional picante sauce.
   Makes 20 appetizers.

Eating On The Roll

On a round-up or trail drive in the Old West, the chuck wagon was the place to eat—the only place. The wagon was outfitted like a ship with drawers and shelves— there was a place for everything—including a cradle-like device called a "cooney" which carried fuel underneath the wagon itself. The basic menu was bacon, beans and fried bread with as occasional jack rabbit or "prairie chicken."

Howdy Neighbors Open House

Ham and Cheese Empañadas (p.12)
Chili con Queso Bites (p.11)
Southwestern Super Chili (p.25)
Rice
Orange and Mango Salad
Cornbread
Assorted Sodas and/or Margarita Punch

Layered Chili Bean Dip

PREP TIME: 15 MINUTES
COOK TIME: 10 MINUTES

1 pound ground beef
1 tablespoon chili powder
1 can (about 16 ounces) black beans, drained
3/4 cup PACE Picante Sauce
1 large tomato, chopped (about 1 1/2 cups)
1 large avocado, peeled, pitted and diced
1 cup shredded Cheddar cheese (4 ounces)
1/4 cup sliced pitted ripe olives

1. In medium skillet over medium-high heat, cook beef and chili powder until beef is browned, stirring to separate meat. Pour off fat.

2. Add beans and picante sauce. Reduce heat to low and heat through. Top with tomato, avocado, cheese, olives and additional picante sauce. Serve with tortilla chips or warmed flour tortillas for dipping.
Makes 7 1/2 cups.

Sausage Stuffed Mushrooms

PREP TIME: 25 MINUTES
COOK TIME: 10 MINUTES

24 medium mushrooms (about 1 pound)
2 tablespoons margarine *or* butter, melted
1/4 pound bulk pork sausage
1 cup PACE Picante Sauce
1/2 cup dry bread crumbs
Chopped fresh cilantro *or* parsley

1. Remove stems from mushrooms. Chop enough stems to make *1 cup* and set aside. Brush mushroom caps with margarine and place top-side down in shallow baking pan. Set aside.

2. In medium skillet over medium-high heat, cook sausage and chopped mushroom stems until sausage is browned, stirring to separate meat.

3. Stir in *1/2 cup* picante sauce and bread crumbs. Mix lightly. Spoon about *1 tablespoon* stuffing mixture into each mushroom cap.

4. Bake at 425°F. for 10 minutes or until mushrooms are heated through. Top each with *1 teaspoon* remaining picante sauce and cilantro.
   Makes 24 appetizers.

TIP: Cut a thin slice from top of each mushroom cap so mushrooms are level.
TIP: Stuffed mushrooms can be prepared through step 3. Cover and refrigerate up to 24 hours. Bake as in step 4.

Double Cheese Crab Dip

PREP TIME: 10 MINUTES
COOK TIME: 15 MINUTES

1 cup PACE Picante Sauce
1 teaspoon chili powder
1 package (8 ounces) cream cheese, softened
1 can (8 ounces) refrigerated pasteurized crab meat
1 cup shredded Cheddar cheese (4 ounces)
1/4 cup sliced pitted ripe olives
Fresh thyme for garnish

1. Mix picante sauce and chili powder. Spread cream cheese in 9-inch pie plate. Top with picante sauce mixture, crab meat, Cheddar cheese and olives.

2. Bake at 350°F. for 15 minutes or until hot. Top with additional picante sauce. Garnish with thyme. Serve with pita triangles, tortilla chips or fresh vegetables for dipping. **Makes about 3 cups.**

TIP: To soften cream cheese, remove wrapper and place on microwave-safe plate. Microwave on HIGH 15 seconds.

Hot 'n' Honeyed Chicken Wings

PREP TIME: 15 MINUTES
COOK TIME: 55 MINUTES

1 cup PACE Picante Sauce
1/4 cup honey
1/2 teaspoon ground ginger
12 chicken wings (about 2 pounds)

1. Mix picante sauce, honey and ginger. Set aside.

2. Cut tips off wings and discard or save for another use. Cut wings in half at joints to make 24 pieces. Add to picante sauce mixture and toss to coat.

3. Place chicken mixture in foil-lined shallow-sided baking pan. Bake at 400°F. for 55 minutes or until chicken is glazed and no longer pink, turning and brushing often with sauce during last 30 minutes of baking.
Makes 24 appetizers.

Top Of The Heap. PACE Picante Sauce—available in extra-mild, mild, medium and hot varieties—is the number 1 selling Mexican sauce in America.

Beef-on-a-Stick

PREP TIME: 15 MINUTES
COOK TIME: 10 MINUTES

1 pound boneless beef sirloin steak, 3/4 inch thick
3/4 cup PACE Picante Sauce
2 tablespoons vegetable oil
1 tablespoon lemon juice
1/8 teaspoon garlic powder *or* 1 clove garlic, minced
Green onion for garnish

1. Slice beef into thin strips.

2. Mix picante sauce, oil, lemon juice and garlic powder. Add beef and toss to coat.

3. On 24 short skewers, thread beef accordion-style. Reserve picante sauce mixture. Place skewers on lightly oiled grill rack over medium-hot coals. Grill uncovered to desired doneness (allow 10 minutes for medium), turning and brushing often with reserved picante sauce mixture. Discard remaining picante sauce mixture.

4. Serve with additional picante sauce. Garnish with green onion.
Makes 24 appetizers.

Broiled Beef-on-a-Stick: Prepare as in steps 1 and 2. In step 3 place skewers on rack in broiler pan. Broil 4 inches from heat to desired doneness (allow 10 minutes for medium), turning and brushing often with reserved picante sauce mixture. Discard remaining picante sauce mixture. Serve with additional picante sauce. Garnish with green onions

Pepperoni Tortilla Pizzas

PREP TIME: 10 MINUTES
COOK TIME: 10 MINUTES

1/2 cup PACE Picante Sauce
1 large tomato, chopped (about 1 1/2 cups)
1/2 teaspoon dried oregano leaves, crushed
6 flour tortillas (8-inch)
1/2 cup chopped pepperoni
1/2 cup chopped green pepper
1 1/2 cups shredded mozzarella cheese (6 ounces)

1. Mix picante sauce, tomato and oregano. Place tortillas on
   2 baking sheets. Top each tortilla with about *1/4 cup*
   picante sauce mixture. Spread to within 1/2 inch of edge.
   Top with pepperoni, pepper and cheese.

2. Bake at 400°F. for 10 minutes or until hot. Cut each pizza
   into 4 wedges. Serve with additional picante sauce.
   Makes 24 appetizers.

Pepperoni Tortilla Pizzas (left, page 17)
and Beef-on-a-Stick (right, page 16).

Bean and Cheese Quesadillas

PREP TIME: 15 MINUTES
COOK TIME: 10 MINUTES

1 can (about 16 ounces) refried beans
1/2 cup PACE Picante Sauce
12 flour tortillas (8-inch)
1 cup shredded Monterey Jack cheese (4 ounces)
2 green onions, sliced (about 1/4 cup)
Fresh cilantro for garnish

1. Mix beans and picante sauce.

2. Place *6* tortillas on 2 baking sheets. Top each tortilla with about *1/3 cup* bean mixture. Spread to within 1/2 inch of edge. Top with cheese and onions. Moisten edges of tortillas with water. Top with remaining tortillas. Press edges together.

3. Bake at 400°F. for 10 minutes or until hot. Cut each quesadilla into 4 wedges. Garnish with cilantro. Serve with additional picante sauce.
Makes 24 appetizers.

Fiesta Tortilla Roll-Ups

PREP TIME: 20 MINUTES
CHILL TIME: 30 MINUTES

1 package (8 ounces) light cream cheese, softened
1/2 cup PACE Picante Sauce
1 green onion, chopped (about 2 tablespoons)
6 flour tortillas (8-inch)
1 cup shredded spinach leaves *or* romaine lettuce
3 thin slices cooked turkey breast (about 3 ounces),
cut in half
1/4 cup chopped pimiento *or* roasted sweet peppers

1. Stir cream cheese until smooth. Stir in picante sauce and onion. Top each tortilla with about *1/4 cup* cheese mixture. Spread to edge. Top each with spinach, *1/2 slice* turkey and *2 teaspoons* pimiento. Tightly roll up like a jelly roll. Place seam-side down in large shallow dish. Cover and refrigerate at least 30 minutes.

2. Cut each roll into 6 slices. Secure each slice with toothpicks. Serve with additional picante sauce.
Makes 36 appetizers.

Nutritional Values Per Appetizer: Calories 43, Total Fat 2g, Saturated Fat 1g, Cholesterol 4mg, Sodium 147mg, Total Carbohydrate 5g, Dietary Fiber 0g, Protein 2g

Grilled Eggplant and Chips

PREP TIME: 10 MINUTES
COOK TIME: 15 MINUTES

3/4 cup PACE Picante Sauce
1/4 cup prepared Italian salad dressing
1 medium eggplant (about 1 pound), sliced 1/2 inch thick
1 medium onion, thickly sliced (about 3/4 cup)
1 tablespoon chopped fresh cilantro
1/8 teaspoon garlic powder *or* 1 clove garlic, minced

1. Mix picante sauce and dressing.

2. Place eggplant and onion on lightly oiled grill rack over medium-hot coals. Grill uncovered 15 minutes or until vegetables are tender, turning and brushing often with picante sauce mixture. Chop eggplant and onion.

3. In medium bowl mix remaining picante sauce mixture, cilantro and garlic powder. Add eggplant and onion and toss until evenly coated. Serve with tortilla chips for dipping.

Broiled Eggplant and Chips: Prepare as in step 1. In step 2 place eggplant and onion on rack in broiler pan. Broil 4 inches from heat 15 minutes or until vegetables are tender, turning and brushing often with picante sauce mixture. Chop eggplant and onion. Proceed as in step 3.

Black Bean Bonanza Dip

PREP TIME: 10 MINUTES
COOK TIME: 5 MINUTES

1 can (about 16 ounces) black beans, rinsed and drained
3/4 cup PACE Picante Sauce
1 teaspoon ground cumin
1/4 teaspoon garlic powder *or* 2 cloves garlic, minced
1 medium tomato, chopped (about 1 cup)
1/4 cup light sour cream
1 tablespoon chopped fresh cilantro

1. In 2-quart saucepan mash *half* the beans. Add picante sauce, cumin, garlic powder and remaining beans. Over medium heat, heat through.

2. Top with tomato, sour cream and cilantro. Serve with fresh vegetables or baked tortilla chips for dipping.
Serves 12.

 Nutritional Values Per Serving: Calories 54, Total Fat 1g, Saturated Fat 0g, Cholesterol 2mg, Sodium 184mg, Total Carbohydrate 9g, Dietary Fiber 1g, Protein 3g

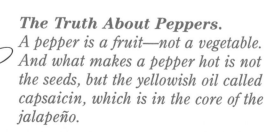

The Truth About Peppers.
A pepper is a fruit—not a vegetable. And what makes a pepper hot is not the seeds, but the yellowish oil called capsaicin, which is in the core of the jalapeño.

Spiced Shrimp in Lettuce Rolls

PREP TIME: 20 MINUTES

1/2 cup PACE Picante Sauce
1 tablespoon lime juice
1 tablespoon chopped fresh cilantro
1 teaspoon minced fresh ginger
1/8 teaspoon garlic powder *or* 1 clove garlic, minced
1 pound medium shrimp, cooked, peeled and
** deveined**
2 medium carrots, shredded (about 1 cup)
12 iceberg lettuce leaves

1. Mix picante sauce, lime juice, cilantro, ginger and garlic powder. Add shrimp and carrots. Toss to coat.

2. Dip each lettuce leaf in hot water to soften. Immediately dip in cold water and drain on paper towels. Spoon *1/4 cup* shrimp mixture into center of each lettuce leaf. Fold lettuce around filling. Secure with toothpick if needed. **Makes 12 appetizers.**

 Nutritional Values Per Appetizer: Calories 34, Total Fat 0g, Saturated Fat 0g, Cholesterol 50mg, Sodium 135mg, Total Carbohydrate 2g, Dietary Fiber 1g, Protein 6g

TIP: Use green onion strips instead of toothpicks to secure rolls.

Spiced Shrimp in Lettuce Rolls (left, page 21)
and Black Bean Bonanza Dip (right, page 20).

Soups, Chilies & Stews

Texas-Style Chili

PREP TIME: 5 MINUTES
COOK TIME: 25 MINUTES

2 pounds ground beef
1 tablespoon chili powder
1 teaspoon ground cumin
1/2 teaspoon salt
1/4 teaspoon garlic powder *or* **2 cloves garlic, minced**
3 tablespoons all-purpose flour
2 cups water
1 cup PACE Picante Sauce
Chopped onions, shredded Cheddar cheese and
   chopped fresh cilantro

1. In large saucepan over medium-high heat, cook beef, chili powder, cumin, salt and garlic powder until beef is browned, stirring to separate meat. Pour off fat.

2. Add flour and cook 1 minute, stirring constantly. Gradually stir in water and picante sauce. Cook until mixture boils and thickens, stirring occasionally. Reduce heat to low. Cook 15 minutes, stirring occasionally. Serve with onions, cheese, cilantro and additional picante sauce.
Serves 6.

Souper Topper
Spoon PACE Picante Sauce on top of your favorite cheese, chicken or bean soup.

Picante Pork Stew (left, page 24) and Texas-Style Chili (right, page 23).

The Great Chili Debate
Beans or no beans? Tomatoes or not? Chunks of meat or ground beef? Chili-lovers everywhere have a point of view. Where they hail from usually determines which version they believe is "right." In truth, the authentic version is from Mexico —"Chili con Carne." What it has in common with all versions of chili is meat and chili powder. And like all homey fare it is pronounced "good" if it tastes great. With the help of PACE, any bowl of chili is a winner.

Picante Pork Stew

PREP TIME: 20 MINUTES
COOK TIME: 25 MINUTES

1 pound boneless pork loin
3 tablespoons cornstarch
1 can (14 1/2 ounces) SWANSON Vegetable Broth
2 tablespoons vegetable oil
4 cups cut-up fresh vegetables*
1/2 cup PACE Picante Sauce

1. Slice pork into very thin strips. In cup mix cornstarch and broth until smooth. Set aside.

2. In Dutch oven over medium-high heat, heat *half* the oil. Add pork in 2 batches and cook until browned, stirring often. Set pork aside.

3. Reduce heat to medium. Add remaining oil. Add vegetables and cook until tender-crisp. Pour off fat.

4. Add picante sauce. Stir cornstarch mixture and add. Cook until mixture boils and thickens, stirring constantly. Return pork to pan and heat through.
   Serves 4.

* Asparagus cut into 2-inch pieces, red pepper strips, sliced onions

TIP: To make slicing easier, freeze pork 1 hour.

Taco Twist Soup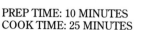

PREP TIME: 10 MINUTES
COOK TIME: 25 MINUTES

1 pound ground beef
2 teaspoons chili powder
1 teaspoon ground cumin
1 can (14 1/2 ounces) SWANSON Beef Broth
1 cup PACE Picante Sauce
1 can (14 1/2 ounces) diced tomatoes in juice
1 cup dry corkscrew macaroni
Sour cream for garnish

1. In large saucepan over medium-high heat, cook beef, chili powder and cumin until beef is browned, stirring to separate meat. Pour off fat.

2. Add broth, picante sauce and tomatoes. Heat to a boil. Stir in macaroni. Reduce heat to medium. Cook 15 minutes or until macaroni is done, stirring occasionally. Garnish with sour cream.
   Serves 4.

Fresh Facts: PACE uses over 30 million pounds of fresh peppers every year. They go from field to sauce in under 10 days.

Southwestern Super Chili

PREP TIME: 10 MINUTES
COOK TIME: 35 MINUTES

1 tablespoon vegetable oil
1 pound skinless, boneless chicken breasts, cut into
** cubes**
1/2 pound kielbasa, cut into 1/2-inch pieces
1 1/2 cups PACE Picante Sauce
1/2 cup water
1 teaspoon ground cumin
1 can (14 1/2 ounces) whole peeled tomatoes, cut up
1 cup frozen whole kernel corn
1 can (about 15 ounces) pinto beans, drained
Lime slice and fresh cilantro for garnish

1. In Dutch oven over medium-high heat, heat oil. Add chicken and kielbasa in 2 batches and cook until chicken is browned, stirring often. Set chicken and kielbasa aside. Pour off fat.

2. Add picante sauce, water, cumin, tomatoes and corn. Heat to a boil. Return chicken and kielbasa to pan. Reduce heat to low. Cover and cook 20 minutes. Add beans and heat through. Garnish with lime and cilantro.
Serves 6.

Taco Twist Soup (top, page 24) and
Southwestern Super Chili (bottom, page 25).

Chilled Picante Gazpacho

PREP TIME: 15 MINUTES
CHILL TIME: 2 HOURS

1 can (28 ounces) whole peeled tomatoes
3/4 cup PACE Picante Sauce
2 tablespoons lemon juice
1 tablespoon chopped fresh cilantro
1/4 teaspoon garlic powder *or* 2 cloves garlic, minced
1 cup thickly sliced cucumber
1 stalk celery, cut into 1-inch pieces (about 3/4 cup)
1 slice firm white bread
1/4 cup chopped cucumber
Green onions for garnish (optional)

1. In blender or food processor place tomatoes, picante sauce, lemon juice, cilantro, garlic powder, sliced cucumber, celery and bread. Cover and blend until smooth. Refrigerate at least 2 hours.

2. Top with chopped cucumber. Garnish with onion, if desired.
   Serves 4.

 Nutritional Values Per Serving: Calories 97, Total Fat 1g, Saturated Fat 0g, Cholesterol 0mg, Sodium 748mg, Total Carbohydrate 20g, Dietary Fiber 4g, Protein 4g

Pace-Setting Chicken Corn Chowder

PREP TIME: 10 MINUTES
COOK TIME: 10 MINUTES

**1 can (10 3/4 ounces) CAMPBELL'S condensed
Cream of Celery Soup**
1 soup can milk
1/2 cup PACE Picante Sauce
1 can (about 8 ounces) whole kernel corn, drained
1 cup cubed cooked chicken
4 slices bacon, cooked and crumbled
Shredded Cheddar cheese
Sliced green onions

In medium saucepan mix soup, milk, picante sauce, corn,
chicken and bacon. Over medium heat, heat through, stirring
occasionally. Top with cheese and onions. Drizzle with additional picante sauce.
Serves 4.

Say It Like A Cowboy

As people moved their lives Westward, their way of speaking changed too. A few expressions give the flavor of a pioneer's life and language.

Possibles: *The clothing, food and ammunition that a trapper would get in exchange for his pelts.*

Making Meat: *Laying down food—in the form of hunted game—for the winter season.*

Up To Beaver: *A compliment meaning "smart," because one had to be clever to catch a beaver.*

Chicken with Rice Soup

PREP TIME: 10 MINUTES
COOK TIME: 15 MINUTES

2 cans (14 1/2 ounces *each*) SWANSON Chicken Broth
1 medium carrot, sliced (about 1/2 cup)
1/2 cup frozen whole kernel corn
1 cup PACE Picante Sauce
1/4 teaspoon garlic powder *or* 2 cloves garlic, minced
1 can (about 15 ounces) kidney beans, drained
1 1/2 cups cubed cooked chicken
1 1/2 cups hot cooked rice

1. In large saucepan mix broth, carrot and corn. Over medium-high heat, heat to a boil. Reduce heat to low. Cover and cook 5 minutes or until vegetables are tender.

2. Add picante sauce, garlic powder, beans and chicken and heat through.

3. Place rice in individual bowls. Ladle soup into bowls. **Serves 8.**

Quick Southwestern Supper

Chicken with Rice Soup (p.28)
Black Bean and Vegetable Tacos (p.36)
Spinach and Mushroom Salad
Vanilla Ice Cream with Cinnamon
Mexican Hot Chocolate

Chicken Tortilla Soup

PREP TIME: 10 MINUTES
COOK TIME: 15 MINUTES

4 corn tortillas (6-inch), cut into strips
2 cans (14 1/2 ounces *each*)
** SWANSON Chicken Broth**
1/2 cup PACE Picante Sauce
1 teaspoon garlic powder
1 can (14 1/2 ounces) whole peeled tomatoes, cut up
2 medium carrots, shredded (about 1 cup)
1 1/2 cups chopped cooked chicken

1. Bake tortilla strips on baking sheet at 400°F. for 15 minutes or until golden brown.

2. In large saucepan mix broth, picante sauce, garlic powder, tomatoes and carrots. Over medium heat, heat to a boil. Reduce heat to low. Cook 5 minutes. Add chicken and heat through.

3. Place tortilla chips in individual bowls. Ladle soup into bowls.
Serves 4.

Chicken Tortilla Soup (top, page 29) and Chicken with Rice Soup (bottom, page 28).

Quick and Easy Beef Stew

PREP TIME: 10 MINUTES
COOK TIME: 20 MINUTES

2 tablespoons cornstarch
2 tablespoons water
1 tablespoon vegetable oil
1 pound boneless beef sirloin steak, cut into
  1-inch cubes
1 tablespoon chili powder
3/4 cup PACE Picante Sauce
1 can (about 16 ounces) black beans
1 can (about 15 ounces) pinto beans
1 can (about 14 1/2 ounces) stewed tomatoes
Fresh tarragon for garnish

1. In cup mix cornstarch and water until smooth. Set aside.

2. In Dutch oven over medium-high heat, heat oil. Add beef and chili powder and cook until beef is browned, stirring often.

3. Add picante sauce, black beans, pinto beans and tomatoes. Heat to a boil. Return heat to low. Cover and cook 5 minutes or until beef is done.

4. Stir cornstarch mixture and add. Cook until mixture boils and thickens, stirring constantly. Garnish with tarragon. **Serves 6.**

Meatball Chili Stew

PREP TIME: 15 MINUTES
COOK TIME: 25 MINUTES

1 cup PACE Picante Sauce
1 pound ground beef
1/2 cup crushed tortilla chips
1 egg, beaten
1/4 teaspoon garlic powder *or* 2 cloves garlic, minced
1 tablespoon vegetable oil
2 teaspoons chili powder
1 can (28 ounces) whole peeled tomatoes, cut up
1 can (about 15 ounces) kidney beans, drained
Chopped fresh cilantro

1. Mix *1/2 cup* picante sauce, beef, chips, egg and garlic
   powder *thoroughly* and shape *firmly* into 24 (1-inch)
   meatballs.

2. In Dutch oven over medium-high heat, heat oil. Add
   meatballs in 2 batches and cook until evenly browned.
   Set meatballs aside. Pour off fat.

3. Add remaining picante sauce, chili powder, tomatoes and
   beans. Heat to a boil. Return meatballs to pan. Reduce
   heat to low. Cover and cook 10 minutes or until meatballs
   are no longer pink. Top with cilantro and additional
   crushed tortilla chips.
   Serves 6.

Recipe For A New Cuisine

- *Take chilies and tomatoes from North America.*
- *Take onions and garlic from Europe and the Mediterranean.*
- *Combine with a little meat or poultry or cheese.*
- *Mix together in the heart of Texas.*
- *Then serve with tortillas and beans—traditional foods of native Mexicans. That's how Tex-Mex came to be a cuisine. And it is totally unique— a true "melting pot" blend of Spanish-Mexican and European-American foods.*

Picante Onion Soup

PREP TIME: 10 MINUTES
COOK TIME: 30 MINUTES

1/4 cup margarine *or* butter
3 large onions, sliced (about 3 cups)
1/8 teaspoon garlic powder *or* 1 clove garlic, minced
2 1/2 cups tomato juice
1 can (14 1/2 ounces) SWANSON Beef Broth
1/2 cup PACE Picante Sauce
1 cup PEPPERIDGE FARM Home Style Zesty Italian Croutons
1 cup shredded Monterey Jack cheese (4 ounces)

1. In large saucepan over medium heat, heat margarine. Add onions and garlic powder and cook 15 minutes or until golden brown, stirring often.

2. Add tomato juice, broth and picante sauce. Heat to a boil. Reduce heat to low. Cover and cook 10 minutes. Top with croutons and cheese.
   Serves 6.

Two-Bean Soup with Cornbread

PREP TIME: 10 MINUTES
COOK TIME: 25 MINUTES

1 can (14 1/2 ounces) SWANSON Beef Broth
1/2 cup PACE Picante Sauce
1/2 teaspoon dried oregano leaves, crushed
1/8 teaspoon garlic powder *or* 1 clove garlic, minced
1 can (about 16 ounces) black beans
1 can (about 15 ounces) pinto beans
4 servings cornbread
Chopped green onions

1. In large saucepan mix broth, picante sauce, oregano, garlic powder, black beans and pinto beans. Heat to a boil. Reduce heat to low. Cover and cook 20 minutes.

2. Place cornbread in individual bowls. Ladle soup into bowls and sprinkle with onions.
   Serves 4.

> ### *Santa Fe Super Bowl Spread*
>
> **Layered Chili Bean Dip (p.13)**
> **Hot 'n' Honeyed Chicken Wings (p.16)**
> **Two-Bean Soup with Cornbread (p.33)**
> **Texas-Style Chili (p.23)**
> **Rice**
> **Brownies**
> **Assorted Sodas and/or Mexican Beers**

Two-Bean Soup with Cornbread (top, page 33)
and Picante Onion Soup (bottom, page 32).

Southwest Main Dishes

Donna's Creamy Chicken Enchiladas

PREP TIME: 20 MINUTES
COOK TIME: 40 MINUTES

1 can (10 3/4 ounces) CAMPBELL'S condensed
   Cream of Chicken Soup
1 container (8 ounces) sour cream
1 cup PACE Picante Sauce
2 teaspoons chili powder
2 cups chopped cooked chicken
1 cup shredded Monterey Jack cheese (4 ounces)
12 flour tortillas (6-inch)
1 medium tomato, chopped (about 1 cup)
1 green onion, sliced (about 2 tablespoons)

1. Mix soup, sour cream, picante sauce and chili powder.
   Reserve *1 cup*.

2. Mix *1 cup* picante sauce mixture, chicken and cheese.

3. Spread about *1/4 cup* chicken mixture down center of
   each tortilla. Roll up and place seam-side
   down in 3-quart shallow baking dish.

4. Pour remaining picante sauce mixture over
   enchiladas. Cover and bake at 350° F. for
   40 minutes or until hot. Top with additional
   picante sauce, tomato and onion.
   Serves 6.

Trailblazing Toppers
Tacos/Burritos
Top tacos or burritos with PACE Picante Sauce.

Enchiladas
Pour PACE Picante Sauce over enchiladas.

Other Mexican Foods
Serve PACE Picante Sauce alongside your favorite Mexican food.

Donna's Creamy Chicken Encholadas (left, page 35) and Black Bean and Vegetable Tacos (right, page 36).

Black Bean and Vegetable Tacos

PREP TIME: 15 MINUTES
COOK TIME: 15 MINUTES

Vegetable cooking spray
1 medium carrot, shredded (about 1/2 cup)
1 teaspoon chili powder
1/2 cup PACE Picante Sauce
1 can (about 16 ounces) black beans, rinsed and
  drained
1 1/2 cups frozen whole kernel corn
6 flour tortillas (8-inch)
1/2 cup shredded reduced-fat Cheddar cheese
  (2 ounces)
1 cup shredded lettuce
1/4 cup light sour cream

1. Spray medium skillet with cooking spray and heat over
   medium heat 1 minute. Add carrot and chili powder and
   cook until tender.

2. Add picante sauce, beans and corn. Heat to a boil. Reduce
   heat to low and cook 5 minutes or until corn is tender.

3. Warm tortillas according to package directions. Spoon
   1/2 cup bean mixture down center of each tortilla. Top
   with cheese, lettuce and sour cream. Roll up.
   Makes 6 tacos.

Nutritional Values Per Serving: Calories 317, Total Fat 7g, Saturated
Fat 3g, Cholesterol 10mg, Sodium 707mg, Total Carbohydrate 52g,
Dietary Fiber 3g, Protein 14g

Easy Chicken Molé

PREP TIME: 5 MINUTES
COOK TIME: 35 MINUTES

1 tablespoon vegetable oil
6 skinless, boneless chicken breast halves
  (about 1 1/2 pounds)
1 can (15 ounces) tomato sauce
1/2 cup PACE Picante Sauce
1 tablespoon unsweetened cocoa
1 tablespoon packed brown sugar
1 teaspoon ground cumin
1/2 teaspoon ground cinnamon
1/4 teaspoon garlic powder *or* 2 cloves garlic, minced
6 cups hot cooked rice, cooked without salt

1. In medium skillet over medium-high heat, heat oil.
   Add chicken in 2 batches and cook 10 minutes or until
   browned. Set chicken aside.

2. Add tomato sauce, picante sauce, cocoa, sugar, cumin,
   cinnamon and garlic powder. Heat to a boil. Reduce heat
   to low. Cook 5 minutes. Return chicken to pan. Cover and
   cook 5 minutes more or until chicken is no longer pink.
   Serve with rice.
   Serves 6.

Nutritional Values Per Serving: Calories 468, Total Fat 6g, Saturated
Fat 1g, Cholesterol 72mg, Sodium 678mg, Total Carbohydrate
67g, Dietary Fiber 2g, Protein 33g

Chicken Tomatillo Enchiladas

PREP TIME: 25 MINUTES
COOK TIME: 40 MINUTES

1 package (8 ounces) cream cheese, softened
1 3/4 cups PACE Picante Sauce
2 cups chopped cooked chicken
2 cups shredded Monterey Jack cheese (8 ounces)
12 corn tortillas (6-inch)
1 cup tomato purée
2 tablespoons chopped fresh cilantro
1/8 teaspoon garlic powder *or* 1 clove garlic, minced
1 can (about 11 ounces) tomatillos, drained and
    chopped
Fresh cilantro for garnish

1. Stir cream cheese until smooth. Stir in *3/4 cup* picante sauce, chicken and *1 cup* Monterey Jack cheese.

2. Warm tortillas according to package directions. Spoon about *1/4 cup* chicken mixture down center of each tortilla. Roll up and place seam-side down in 3-quart shallow baking dish.

3. Mix remaining picante sauce, tomato purée, cilantro, garlic powder and tomatillos. Pour over enchiladas. Cover and bake at 350°F. for 35 minutes or until hot. Uncover. Top with remaining Monterey Jack cheese. Bake 5 minutes more or until cheese is melted. Garnish with cilantro.
Serves 6.

King Ranch Chicken

PREP TIME: 15 MINUTES
COOK TIME: 40 MINUTES

**1 can (10 3/4 ounces) CAMPBELL'S condensed
  Cream of Mushroom Soup
3/4 cup PACE Picante Sauce
3/4 cup sour cream
1 tablespoon chili powder
2 medium tomatoes, chopped (about 2 cups)
3 cups cubed cooked chicken
12 corn tortillas (6-inch), cut into 1-inch pieces
1 cup shredded Cheddar cheese (4 ounces)
Green onion for garnish**

1. Mix soup, picante sauce, sour cream, chili powder, tomatoes and chicken.

2. In 2-quart shallow baking dish arrange *half* the tortilla pieces. Top with *half* the chicken mixture. Repeat layers. Sprinkle with cheese.

3. Bake at 350° F. for 40 minutes or until hot. Serve with additional picante sauce and garnish with green onion. **Serves 8.**

It's Hot! *People in Los Angeles, west Texas and New Mexico like their salsa hot, with nearly 25% of purchased salsa and picante sauce being hot. The national average for hot is 14%.*

Oven-Fried Chicken Chimichangas

PREP TIME: 20 MINUTES
COOK TIME: 25 MINUTES

2/3 cup PACE Picante Sauce
1 teaspoon ground cumin
1/2 teaspoon dried oregano leaves, crushed
1 1/2 cups chopped cooked chicken
1 cup shredded Cheddar cheese (4 ounces)
2 green onions, chopped (about 1/4 cup)
6 flour tortillas (8-inch)
2 tablespoons margarine *or* butter, melted

1. Mix picante sauce, cumin, oregano, chicken, cheese and onions.

2. Place about *1/2 cup* chicken mixture in center of each tortilla. Fold opposite sides over filling. Roll up from bottom and place seam-side down on baking sheet. Brush with margarine.

3. Bake at 400°F. for 25 minutes or until golden. Garnish with additional cheese and green onion. Serve with additional picante sauce.
   Makes 6 chimichangas.

TIP: To melt margarine, remove wrapper and place in microwave-safe cup. Cover and microwave on HIGH 30 seconds.

Y'All Come Reunion

Fiesta Chicken and Rice (p.41)
Picante Macaroni and Cheese (p.66)
Zucchini
Garden Salad with Avocado
Corn Muffins
Rice Pudding with Cinnamon Sugar
Punch and/or White Wine Sangria

Spicy Sausage and Bean Tostadas

PREP TIME: 15 MINUTES
COOK TIME: 15 MINUTES

1/4 pound chorizo sausage, casing removed
1/2 cup PACE Picante Sauce
1 teaspoon chili powder
1 can (about 16 ounces) pinto beans, drained
1 can (14 1/2 ounces) whole peeled tomatoes, drained and cut up
1 medium potato, cooked and cubed (about 1 cup)
Vegetable oil
8 corn tortillas (6-inch)
2 cups shredded lettuce
1 cup shredded Monterey Jack cheese (4 ounces)

1. In large saucepan over medium-high heat, cook sausage until browned, stirring to separate meat. Pour off fat.

2. Reduce heat to medium. Add picante sauce, chili powder, beans, tomatoes and potato. Cook 10 minutes.

3. In small skillet over medium-high heat, heat 1 inch oil. Add tortillas one at a time and cook until crisp. Drain.

4. Top each tortilla with lettuce, about *1/3 cup* sausage mixture and cheese. Serve with additional picante sauce.
Serves 4.

Fiesta Chicken and Rice

PREP TIME: 10 MINUTES
COOK TIME: 30 MINUTES

1 tablespoon vegetable oil
1 cup uncooked regular long-grain white rice
1 can (10 1/2 ounces) CAMPBELL'S condensed
   Chicken Broth
1 cup water
1/2 cup PACE Picante Sauce
1 teaspoon ground cumin
2 medium tomatoes, coarsely chopped (about 2 cups)
1 cup frozen peas
2 green onions, sliced (about 1/4 cup)
2 cups cubed cooked chicken

1. In medium skillet over medium heat, heat oil. Add rice
   and cook until browned, stirring constantly.

2. Stir in broth, water, picante sauce and cumin. Heat to a
   boil. Reduce heat to low. Cover and cook 15 minutes.

3. Stir in tomatoes, peas, onions and chicken. Cover and
   cook 5 minutes more or until rice is done and most of
   liquid is absorbed.
   Serves 4.

*Spicy Sausage and Bean Tostadas (top, page 40) and
Fiesta Chicken and Rice (bottom, page 41).*

Picadillo Stuffed Pepper Casserole

PREP TIME: 20 MINUTES
COOK TIME: 30 MINUTES

1 pound ground beef
1/8 teaspoon garlic powder *or* 1 clove garlic, minced
1 can (about 14 1/2 ounces) stewed tomatoes
1/2 cup PACE Picante Sauce
1 teaspoon ground cumin
1/4 teaspoon ground cinnamon
1/3 cup raisins
1/3 cup toasted slivered almonds
2 medium green peppers, cut into quarters lengthwise
1/2 cup shredded Cheddar cheese (2 ounces)
Fresh basil for garnish

1. In skillet over medium-high heat, cook beef and garlic powder until beef is browned, stirring to separate meat. Pour off fat.

2. Add tomatoes, picante sauce, cumin, cinnamon, raisins and almonds. Reduce heat to low and heat through.

3. Arrange peppers in 2-quart casserole. Spoon beef mixture into pepper-lined casserole.

4. Cover and bake at 400°F. for 25 minutes or until peppers are tender. Uncover. Top with cheese. Bake 5 minutes more or until cheese is melted. Serve with additional picante sauce. Garnish with basil.
Serves 4.

Steak and Pepper Fajitas

PREP TIME: 15 MINUTES
COOK TIME: 15 MINUTES

1 pound boneless beef sirloin steak, 3/4 inch thick
1 cup PACE Picante Sauce
1 tablespoon vegetable oil
2 medium green *or* red peppers, cut into strips
  (about 3 cups)
1 medium red onion, sliced (about 1/2 cup)
1 tablespoon chopped fresh cilantro
8 flour tortillas (6-inch)
1 cup shredded Cheddar cheese (4 ounces)

1. Place steak on rack in broiler pan. Broil 4 inches from heat to desired doneness (allow 15 minutes for medium), turning once and brushing often with *1/3 cup* picante sauce.

2. In medium skillet over medium heat, heat oil. Add peppers and onions and cook until tender-crisp. Add remaining picante sauce and cilantro and heat through.

3. Warm tortillas according to package directions. Slice steak into thin strips and place down center of each tortilla. Top with pepper mixture and cheese. Roll up. Serve with additional picante sauce.
Serves 4.

Grilled Steak and Pepper Fajitas: Grill steak on lightly oiled grill rack over medium-hot coals to desired doneness (allow 15 minutes for medium), turning once and brushing often with *1/3 cup* picante sauce. Proceed as directed in steps 2 and 3.

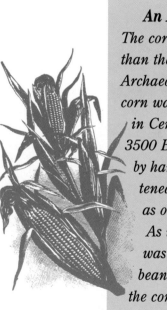

An Ancient Lineage

The corn tortilla is far older than the Mexico of Tex-Mex. Archaeologists tell us that corn was under cultivation in Central America in 3500 B.C. Corn—pounded by hand into a paste, flattened and then baked—is as old as the region itself. As it often is today, it was served then with beans which complement the corn—not only in taste but nutritionally.

Monterey Tortilla Casserole

PREP TIME: 10 MINUTES
COOK TIME: 40 MINUTES

1 cup coarsely crumbled tortilla chips
2 cups cubed cooked turkey *or* chicken
1 can (about 16 ounces) cream-style corn
3/4 cup PACE Picante Sauce
1/2 cup sliced pitted ripe olives
1 cup shredded Cheddar cheese (4 ounces)
Chopped green *or* red pepper
Tortilla chips

1. In 2-quart casserole layer crumbled chips, turkey, corn and picante sauce. Top with olives and cheese.

2. Bake at 350°F. for 40 minutes or until hot. Top with pepper. Serve with chips.
Serves 4.

Cowpoke's Birthday Party

Pepperoni Tortilla Pizzas (p.17)
Cool Chicken and Chips (p.45)
Fresh Vegetables and Dip
Cupcakes
Lemonade and/or Assorted Sodas

Cool Chicken and Chips

PREP TIME: 20 MINUTES

1 cup PACE Picante Sauce
1/2 cup sour cream
2 cups cubed cooked chicken
4 cups tortilla chips
4 cups shredded lettuce (about 1 small head)
1/4 cup sliced pitted ripe olives
2 green onions, sliced (about 1/4 cup)
1/2 cup shredded Cheddar cheese (2 ounces)

1. Mix *1/2 cup* picante sauce, sour cream and chicken.

2. Arrange chips on platter. Top with lettuce, chicken
   mixture, olives, onions and cheese. Drizzle remaining
   picante sauce over top.
   Serves 4.

Beef and Cornbread Bake

PREP TIME: 15 MINUTES
COOK TIME: 30 MINUTES
STAND TIME: 10 MINUTES

1 pound ground beef
1 teaspoon dried oregano leaves, crushed
3/4 cup PACE Picante Sauce
1 can (8 ounces) tomato sauce
1 can (about 16 ounces) whole kernel corn, drained
1/2 cup shredded Cheddar cheese (2 ounces)
1 package (7 1/2 to 8 1/2 ounces) corn muffin mix

1. Preheat oven to 375°F.

2. In medium skillet over medium-high heat, cook beef and oregano until beef is browned, stirring to separate meat. Pour off fat. Add picante sauce, tomato sauce and corn. Reduce heat to low and heat through. Stir in cheese. Pour into 2-quart square baking dish.

3. Prepare corn muffin mix according to package directions. Spread over meat mixture.

4. Bake 25 to 30 minutes or until cornbread topping is deep golden brown and pulls away from the edges of the dish. Let stand 10 minutes.
Serves 6.

Sausage Tostada Grande

PREP TIME: 20 MINUTES
COOK TIME: 30 MINUTES

1/2 pound Italian pork sausage, casing removed
1 can (14 1/2 ounces) whole peeled tomatoes, drained and cut up
3/4 cup PACE Picante Sauce
1 teaspoon ground cumin
12 corn tortillas (6-inch)
1 cup shredded Monterey Jack cheese (4 ounces)
2 cups shredded lettuce
1 medium tomato, chopped (about 1 cup)
Sliced pitted ripe olives for garnish

1. In medium skillet over medium-high heat, cook sausage until browned, stirring to separate meat. Pour off fat. Add canned tomatoes, picante sauce and cumin. Heat to a boil. Reduce heat to medium. Cook 10 minutes.

2. Place tortillas on 14-inch pizza pan or large baking sheet, overlapping to form a 14-inch round. Spread sausage mixture over tortillas to within 1/2 inch of edge. Bake at 350°F. for 25 minutes.

3. Top with cheese. Bake 5 minutes more or until cheese is melted. Top with lettuce and chopped tomato. Cut into wedges. Serve with additional picante sauce. Garnish with olives.
Serves 4.

Trim-a-Tree Fiesta

Pace Picante Sauce with Guacamole and Chips
Enchiladas Fantasticas (p.48)
King Ranch Chicken (p.38)
Spanish-Style Rice (p.98)
Caramel Flan
Punch and/or Sangria

Enchiladas Fantasticas

PREP TIME: 25 MINUTES
COOK TIME: 40 MINUTES

1 tablespoon vegetable oil
1 pound ground turkey
1 1/2 cups PACE Picante Sauce
1 1/2 teaspoons ground cumin
1 package (about 10 ounces) frozen chopped spinach, thawed and well drained
1 package (8 ounces) cream cheese, cubed
12 flour tortillas (6-inch)
1 can (14 1/2 ounces) diced tomatoes in juice
1 cup shredded Cheddar cheese (4 ounces)

1. In medium skillet over medium-high heat, heat oil. Add turkey and cook until no longer pink, stirring to separate meat. Pour off fat.

2. Add *1 cup* picante sauce, cumin and spinach. Heat to a boil. Reduce heat to low. Cook 5 minutes. Add cream cheese and stir until melted.

3. Spread about *1/3 cup* spinach mixture down center of each tortilla. Roll up and place seam-side down in 3-quart shallow baking dish.

4. Combine tomatoes and remaining picante sauce. Spoon over enchiladas. Cover and bake at 350°F. for 35 minutes or until hot. Uncover. Top with cheese. Bake 5 minutes more or until cheese is melted. Serve with additional picante sauce.
Serves 6.

Seven-Layer Meatless Tortilla Pie

PREP TIME: 20 MINUTES
COOK TIME: 40 MINUTES

2 cans (about 15 ounces *each*) pinto beans, drained
1 cup PACE Picante Sauce
1/4 teaspoon garlic powder *or* 2 cloves garlic, minced
2 tablespoons chopped fresh cilantro
1 can (about 16 ounces) black beans, drained
1 small tomato, chopped (about 1/2 cup)
7 flour tortillas (8-inch)
2 cups shredded Cheddar cheese (8 ounces)

1. Mash pinto beans. Stir in *3/4 cup* picante sauce and garlic powder.

2. Mix remaining picante sauce, cilantro, black beans and tomato.

3. Place *1* tortilla on baking sheet. Spread *3/4 cup* pinto bean mixture over tortilla to within 1/2 inch of edge. Top with *1/4 cup* cheese. Top with *1* tortilla and *2/3 cup* black bean mixture. Top with *1/4 cup* cheese. Repeat layers twice more. Top with remaining tortilla and spread with remaining pinto bean mixture. Cover with foil.

4. Bake at 400°F. for 40 minutes or until hot. Uncover. Top with remaining cheese. Cut into wedges. Serve with additional picante sauce. Garnish with additional cilantro. **Serves 6.**

Everyday Family Favorites

Ginger Spicy Chicken

PREP TIME: 15 MINUTES
COOK TIME: 25 MINUTES

1 can (about 20 ounces) pineapple chunks in juice
1 tablespoon cornstarch
1 tablespoon sugar
1/2 teaspoon ground ginger
2 teaspoons soy sauce
1/2 cup PACE Picante Sauce
Vegetable cooking spray
2 medium green *or* red peppers, cut into strips
    (about 3 cups)
1 pound skinless, boneless chicken breasts, cut into strips
4 cups hot cooked rice, cooked without salt
Fresh parsley for garnish

1. Drain pineapple, reserving juice. In cup mix cornstarch, sugar, ginger, soy, picante sauce and reserved pineapple juice until smooth. Set aside.

2. Spray medium skillet with cooking spray and heat over medium heat 1 minute. Add peppers and stir-fry until tender-crisp. Set aside.

3. Remove pan from heat. Spray with cooking spray and increase heat to medium-high. Add chicken in 2 batches and stir-fry until browned. Set chicken aside.

4. Stir cornstarch mixture and add to pan. Cook until mixture boils and thickens, stirring constantly. Add pineapple. Return chicken and peppers to pan and heat through. Serve over rice. Garnish with parsley.
Serves 4.

Nutritional Values Per Serving: Calories 472, Total Fat 4g, Saturated Fat 1g, Cholesterol 72mg, Sodium 460mg, Total Carbohydrate 75g, Dietary Fiber 3g, Protein 33g

Tex-Italian Pasta Fiesta (left, page 64) and Ginger Spicy Chicken (right, page 51).

Picante Sauce: It's A Family Affair

It's conventional wisdom that no one in any family can agree on the perfect level of heat for a favorite dish. That's why the cook who uses PACE Mild and puts jars of PACE Medium and PACE Hot sauces on the table is sure to please everyone. Or better yet—let everyone please himself.

Get Your Chicken Kickin'!
Serve baked, grilled, broiled or fried chicken with PACE Picante Sauce .

Skillet Chicken and Rice

PREP TIME: 10 MINUTES
COOK TIME: 40 MINUTES

1 teaspoon ground cumin
1/8 teaspoon garlic powder
1 pound skinless, boneless chicken breasts,
   cut into strips
2 tablespoons vegetable oil
1 cup uncooked regular long-grain white rice
1 can (10 1/2 ounces) CAMPBELL'S condensed
   Chicken Broth
1 1/4 cups water
1/2 cup PACE Picante Sauce
2 cups frozen mixed vegetables

1. Mix cumin and garlic powder. Sprinkle both sides of chicken with cumin mixture.

2. In medium skillet over medium-high heat, heat *half* the oil. Add chicken in 2 batches and cook until browned, stirring often. Set chicken aside.

3. Reduce heat to medium. Heat remaining oil. Add rice and cook until browned, stirring constantly. Stir in broth, water and picante sauce. Heat to a boil. Reduce heat to low. Cover and cook 10 minutes.

4. Stir in vegetables. Return chicken to pan. Cover and cook 10 to 15 minutes more or until rice is done and most of liquid is absorbed.
Serves 4.

Cowboy Etiquette

Cowboys had their own "family dinner" rules. They were laid down by the cook. All of the cowboys on the trail wanted to keep the cook happy, so these rules were law.

- *No one eats until the cook calls.*
- *Eat first. Talk later.*
- *Don't take the last serving unless you're sure you're the last to eat.*

"Grande"-Style Dad's Day Dinner

Beef-on-a-Stick (p.16)
Picante Chicken Italiano (p.53)
Spinach and Orange Salad
Pepperidge Farm Garlic Bread
Cinnamon Chocolate Mousse
Iced Tea and/or Frozen Margaritas

Picante Chicken Italiano

PREP TIME: 10 MINUTES
COOK TIME: 20 MINUTES

1 egg *or* 2 egg whites
2 tablespoons water
6 skinless, boneless chicken breast halves
(about 1 1/2 pounds)
3/4 cup Italian-seasoned dry bread crumbs
2 tablespoons margarine *or* butter, melted
1 1/2 cups PREGO Traditional Spaghetti Sauce
3/4 cup PACE Picante Sauce
6 cups hot cooked spaghetti (about 12 ounces dry)

1. Mix egg and water in shallow dish. Dip chicken into egg mixture. Coat with bread crumbs.

2. Place chicken on baking sheet. Drizzle with margarine. Bake at 400°F. for 20 minutes or until chicken is no longer pink.

3. In small saucepan mix spaghetti sauce and picante sauce. Heat through. Serve with chicken and spaghetti.
Serves 6.

Easy Chicken and Pasta

PREP TIME: 10 MINUTES
COOK TIME: 20 MINUTES

**3 cups dry corkscrew macaroni *or* 2 1/2 cups dry
  medium tube-shaped macaroni
1/2 pound broccoli, trimmed, cut into 1-inch pieces
  (about 2 cups)
1 medium green *or* red pepper, chopped
  (about 3/4 cup)
1 can (10 3/4 ounces) CAMPBELL'S condensed
  Cream of Mushroom Soup
1/4 cup milk
3/4 cup PACE Picante Sauce
1 1/2 cups cubed cooked chicken
Grated Parmesan cheese**

1. In large saucepan prepare macaroni according to package
   directions. Add broccoli and pepper for last 4 minutes of
   cooking time. Drain in colander.

2. In same pan mix soup, milk, picante sauce, chicken and
   macaroni mixture. Over low heat, heat through, stirring
   occasionally. Top with cheese.
   Serves 4.

Easy Cubed Cooked Chicken
*Substitute 1 can (10 ounces) SWANSON
Chunk White Chicken, drained, for
1 1/2 cups cubed cooked chicken.*

Chicken with Picante Black Bean Sauce

PREP TIME: 10 MINUTES
COOK TIME: 35 MINUTES

2 teaspoons ground cumin
1/2 teaspoon garlic powder
6 skinless, boneless chicken breast halves
(about 1 1/2 pounds)
1 tablespoon vegetable oil
2/3 cup PACE Picante Sauce
1/2 cup diced green *or* red pepper
1 can (about 8 ounces) whole kernel corn, drained
1 can (about 16 ounces) black beans, drained
2 tablespoons chopped fresh cilantro

1. Mix *1 teaspoon* cumin and garlic powder. Sprinkle both sides of chicken with cumin mixture.

2. In medium skillet over medium-high heat, heat oil. Add chicken in 2 batches and cook 10 minutes or until browned. Set chicken aside.

3. Add picante sauce, remaining cumin, pepper, corn and beans. Heat to a boil. Return chicken to pan. Reduce heat to low. Cover and cook 10 minutes or until chicken is no longer pink. Sprinkle with cilantro.
Serves 6.

 Nutritional Values Per Serving: Calories 272, Total Fat 6g, Saturated Fat 1g, Cholesterol 72mg, Sodium 479mg, Total Carbohydrate 21g, Dietary Fiber 1g, Protein 33g

Also pictured on cover.

These Boots Were Made For Workin'

In the 1800s, Cowboys chose carefully and paid dearly for a good pair of boots. A custom-made pair cost $15—half a month's salary. The heel was high and tapered so that it would not slip through the stirrup and it could be dug into the ground when the cowboy worked a calf. Cowboys added spurs to penetrate the matted coats of their ungroomed horses. The long leather tabs for pulling on the boots were named after the mule ears they resembled.

Lone Star Luncheon

Fresh Fruit Compote
Chicken Marinara with Pasta (p.57)
Romaine and Avocado Salad
Pepperidge Farm Bread Sticks
Orange Sherbet with Assorted
Pepperidge Farm Cookies
Iced Flavored Tea

Picante Rice and Beans

PREP TIME: 15 MINUTES
COOK TIME: 15 MINUTES

Vegetable cooking spray
2 medium zucchini, cut in half lengthwise and sliced (about 2 cups)
1 teaspoon ground cumin
1/4 teaspoon garlic powder *or* 2 cloves garlic, minced
3/4 cup PACE Picante Sauce
1 medium tomato, coarsely chopped (about 1 cup)
1 cup frozen whole kernel corn
1 can (about 15 ounces) pinto beans, rinsed and drained
4 cups hot cooked rice, cooked without salt
1/2 cup shredded reduced-fat Cheddar cheese (2 ounces)
2 green onions, sliced (about 1/4 cup)

1. Spray medium skillet with cooking spray and heat over medium heat 1 minute. Add zucchini, cumin and garlic powder and cook until tender-crisp.

2. Add *1/2 cup* picante sauce, tomato, corn and beans. Heat to a boil. Reduce heat to low. Cover and cook 5 minutes or until vegetables are tender, stirring often.

3. Serve over rice. Top with remaining picante sauce, cheese and onions.
Serves 4.

Nutritional Values Per Serving: Calories 494, Total Fat 4g, Saturated Fat 2g, Cholesterol 10mg, Sodium 462mg, Total Carbohydrate 95g, Dietary Fiber 11g, Protein 20g

Chicken Marinara with Pasta

PREP TIME: 10 MINUTES
COOK TIME: 20 MINUTES

1 tablespoon vegetable oil
1 pound skinless, boneless chicken breasts, cut into
cubes
1/4 teaspoon garlic powder *or* 2 cloves garlic, minced
2 cups PREGO Traditional Spaghetti Sauce
1 cup PACE Picante Sauce
1 jar (about 4 1/2 ounces) sliced mushrooms, drained
4 cups hot cooked linguine (about 8 ounces dry)
Grated Parmesan cheese

1. In medium skillet over medium heat, heat oil. Add chicken
   and garlic powder and cook 5 minutes, stirring often.

2. Add spaghetti sauce, picante sauce and mushrooms. Heat
   to a boil. Reduce heat to low. Cook 10 minutes or until
   chicken is no longer pink. Serve over linguine with cheese.
   Serves 4.

Chicken Olive Calzones

PREP TIME: 20 MINUTES
COOK TIME: 10 MINUTES

1 package (10 ounces) refrigerated pizza dough
1 egg
1 tablespoon water
3/4 cup PACE Picante Sauce
1 1/2 teaspoons chopped fresh oregano *or*
    1/2 teaspoon dried oregano leaves, crushed
1 cup chopped cooked chicken
1/2 cup shredded Cheddar cheese (2 ounces)
2 tablespoons chopped Spanish pimento-stuffed olives
Grated Parmesan cheese

1. Preheat oven to 425°F. Unroll pizza dough on lightly floured surface and pat into 15-by10-inch rectangle. Cut into 6 (5-inch) squares. Mix egg and water and set aside.

2. Mix picante sauce, oregano, chicken, Cheddar cheese and olives.

3. Spoon about *1/4 cup* chicken mixture in center of each square. Brush edges of squares with egg mixture. Fold squares to form triangles. Pinch edges together. Place on greased baking sheet. Brush with egg mixture. Sprinkle with Parmesan cheese.

4. Bake 10 minutes or until browned. Serve with additional picante sauce. Garnish with additional olives and oregano. **Makes 6 calzones.**

Szechuan-Style Chicken and Broccoli

PREP TIME: 15 MINUTES
COOK TIME: 25 MINUTES

1 tablespoon cornstarch
3/4 cup PACE Picante Sauce
2 tablespoons soy sauce
1 teaspoon sugar
2 tablespoons vegetable oil
1 pound skinless, boneless chicken breasts, cut into cubes
2 cups broccoli flowerets
1 medium green *or* red pepper, cut into 1-inch pieces (about 1 cup)
1 medium onion, cut into wedges
4 cups hot cooked rice

1. In cup mix cornstarch, picante sauce, soy and sugar until smooth. Set aside.

2. In medium skillet over medium-high heat, heat *half* the oil. Add chicken in 2 batches and stir-fry until browned. Set chicken aside.

3. Reduce heat to medium. Add remaining oil. Add broccoli, pepper and onion and stir-fry until tender-crisp.

4. Stir cornstarch mixture and add. Cook until mixture boils and thickens, stirring constantly. Return chicken to pan. Reduce heat to low. Cover and cook 5 minutes or until chicken is no longer pink. Serve over rice.
Serves 4.

Thrills & Spills

The instinct of an untamed horse is to buck, plunge and kick violently if anything is on its back. In the Old West, nothing was more entertaining to seasoned cowboys than watching an inexperienced cowboy or "greenhorn" trying to "break" a wild horse. Over the years, the taming of wild horses evolved into the entertainment known as bronco busting. As a form of rodeo entertainment today, it requires the cowboy to use a hornless saddle, hold a single rein in one hand and stay on for a full 8 seconds.

Tex-Mex Teen Party

Pace Picante Sauce with Chips
Cheesy Chicken Pizza (p.61)
Chili Mac (p.73)
Fresh Vegetables with Dip
Make-Your-Own Ice Cream Sundaes
Cider and/or Lemonade

Szechuan Peanut Chicken

PREP TIME: 10 MINUTES
COOK TIME: 15 MINUTES

1 pound skinless, boneless chicken breasts, cut into strips
2 tablespoons soy sauce
1 teaspoon ground ginger *or* 1 tablespoon minced fresh ginger
1/8 teaspoon garlic powder *or* 1 clove garlic, minced
1 tablespoon vegetable oil
1/2 cup PACE Picante Sauce
2 tablespoons creamy peanut butter
3 green onions, thickly sliced (about 3/4 cup)
4 cups hot cooked thin spaghetti (about 8 ounces dry)
Sliced green onions

1. Mix chicken, soy, ginger and garlic powder.

2. In medium skillet over medium-high heat, heat oil. Add chicken mixture in 2 batches and stir-fry until browned. Set chicken aside.

3. Reduce heat to medium. Add picante sauce, peanut butter and onions and stir until smooth. Return chicken to pan and heat through. Serve over spaghetti. Sprinkle with additional onions.
Serves 4.

Cheesy Chicken Pizza

PREP TIME: 15 MINUTES
COOK TIME: 15 MINUTES

1 package (10 ounces) refrigerated pizza dough
1/2 cup PACE Picante Sauce
1/2 cup PREGO Traditional Spaghetti Sauce
1 cup chopped cooked chicken
1/2 cup sliced pitted ripe olives
2 green onions, sliced (about 1/4 cup)
1 cup shredded mozzarella cheese (4 ounces)

1. Preheat oven to 425°F. Grease 12-inch pizza pan or baking
   sheet. Unroll pizza dough and pat into 12-inch round,
   pinching edge to form rim.

2. Mix picante sauce and spaghetti sauce. Spread over crust
   to within 1/4 inch of edge. Top with chicken, olives, onions
   and cheese. Bake 15 minutes or until cheese is melted and
   crust is golden.
   Serves 4.

TIP: For crisper crust, bake pizza dough 5 minutes before topping as
directed in step 2.

Texas Two-Step Chicken Picante

PREP TIME: 5 MINUTES
COOK TIME: 15 MINUTES

1 1/2 cups PACE Picante Sauce (12 ounces)
3 tablespoons packed light brown sugar
1 tablespoon Dijon-style mustard
4 skinless, boneless chicken breast halves
 (about 1 pound)
3 cups hot cooked rice

1. Mix picante sauce, sugar and mustard.

2. Place chicken on lightly oiled grill rack over medium-hot coals. Grill uncovered 15 minutes or until chicken is no longer pink, turning and brushing often with *1/2 cup* picante sauce mixture. Heat remaining sauce to a boil and serve with chicken and rice.
Serves 4.

Easy Oven Chicken Picante: Prepare as in step 1. In step 2 place chicken in 2-quart shallow baking dish. Pour picante sauce mixture over chicken. Bake at 400°F. for 20 minutes or until chicken is no longer pink. Serve with rice.

Kid-Pleasing Chicken Picante:
Use the mild variety of PACE Picante Sauce.

Chicken and Peppers Pie

PREP TIME: 10 MINUTES
COOK TIME: 30 MINUTES

**1 can (10 3/4 ounces) CAMPBELL'S condensed
  Cream of Chicken Soup**
1/2 cup PACE Picante Sauce
1/2 cup sour cream
2 teaspoons chili powder
**1 jar (7 ounces) whole roasted sweet peppers,
  drained and cut into strips**
4 green onions, sliced (about 1/2 cup)
3 cups cubed cooked chicken
**1 package (11 1/2 ounces) refrigerated cornbread
  twists**
Fresh sage for garnish

1. In 2-quart shallow baking dish mix soup, picante sauce, sour
   cream, chili powder, peppers, onions and chicken.

2. Bake at 400°F. for 15 minutes or until hot.

3. Stir. Separate bread twists into 16 strips. Arrange strips, lat-
   tice-fashion, over chicken mixture, overlapping strips as
   necessary to fit. Bake 15 minutes more or until bread is
   golden. Garnish with sage and additional roasted peppers.
   Serves 6.

Cinco de Mayo Celebration

Double Cheese Crab Dip (p.15)
Sausage Stuffed Mushrooms (p.14)
Tex-Italian Pasta Fiesta (p.64)
Garden Salad
Cornbread
Buñelos or Sugar Cookies with Ice Cream
Punch and/or Sangria

Tex-Italian Pasta Fiesta

PREP TIME: 25 MINUTES
COOK TIME: 35 MINUTES

1 package (8 ounces) cream cheese, softened
1/2 cup milk
1 teaspoon dried oregano leaves, crushed
1 package (about 10 ounces) frozen chopped spinach, thawed and *well drained*
1 pound ground beef
1/4 teaspoon garlic powder *or* 2 cloves garlic, minced
2 cups PACE Picante Sauce
1 can (15 ounces) tomato sauce
1 tablespoon chili powder
5 cups hot cooked medium tube-shaped macaroni
1 cup shredded mozzarella cheese (4 ounces)

1. Stir cream cheese until smooth. Stir in milk, oregano and spinach. Set aside.

2. In medium skillet over medium-high heat, cook beef and garlic powder until beef is browned, stirring to separate meat. Pour off fat. Stir in picante sauce, tomato sauce, chili powder and macaroni.

3. In 3-quart shallow baking dish spoon *half* the macaroni mixture. Top with spinach mixture and remaining macaroni mixture. Cover.

4. Bake at 400°F. for 30 minutes or until hot. Uncover and sprinkle with mozzarella cheese. Bake 5 minutes more or until cheese is melted. Serve with additional picante sauce. **Serves 8.**

Picante Shrimp 'n' Peppers Pasta

PREP TIME: 15 MINUTES
COOK TIME: 20 MINUTES

1 tablespoon vegetable oil
2 small green *or* yellow peppers, cut into strips
(about 2 cups)
1 cup sliced mushrooms (about 3 ounces)
1 teaspoon dried basil leaves, crushed
1/4 teaspoon garlic powder *or* 2 cloves garlic, minced
1 cup PACE Picante Sauce
2 medium tomatoes, coarsely chopped (about 2 cups)
1 pound medium shrimp, peeled and deveined
3 1/4 cups cooked medium tube-shaped macaroni
(about 2 cups dry)

1. In medium skillet over medium heat, heat oil. Add
   peppers, mushrooms, basil and garlic powder and cook
   until tender-crisp.

2. Add picante sauce, tomatoes and shrimp. Heat to a boil.
   Reduce heat to low. Cook 5 minutes or until shrimp turn
   pink. Add macaroni and heat through.
   Serves 4.

Nutritional Values Per Serving: Calories 314, Total Fat 6g, Saturated
Fat 1g, Cholesterol 158mg, Sodium 631mg, Total Carbohydrate 41g,
Dietary Fiber 5g, Protein 24g

Picante Macaroni and Cheese

PREP TIME: 20 MINUTES
COOK TIME: 30 MINUTES

**1 can (10 3/4 ounces) CAMPBELL'S condensed
 Cream of Mushroom Soup
1/2 cup PACE Picante Sauce
2 cups shredded Cheddar cheese (8 ounces)
3 cups hot cooked elbow macaroni
 (about 1 1/2 cups dry)
1/2 cup crumbled tortilla chips
Fresh cilantro for garnish**

1. In 1 1/2-quart casserole mix soup, picante sauce,
   1 1/2 cups cheese and macaroni.

2. Bake at 400° F. for 25 minutes or until hot.

3. Stir. Sprinkle with chips and remaining cheese. Bake
   5 minutes more or until cheese is melted. Serve with
   additional picante sauce. Garnish with cilantro.
   Serves 4.

Chili-Topped Potatoes

PREP TIME: 5 MINUTES
COOK TIME: 15 MINUTES

1 pound ground beef
1 tablespoon chili powder
1 cup PACE Picante Sauce
4 hot baked potatoes, split
Shredded Cheddar cheese
Chopped fresh chives for garnish

1. In medium skillet over medium-high heat, cook beef and
   chili powder until beef is browned, stirring to separate
   meat. Pour off fat.

2. Add picante sauce. Reduce heat to low and heat through.

3. Serve over potatoes. Top with cheese. Garnish with chives.
   Serves 4.

TIP: To bake potatoes, pierce potatoes with fork. Bake at 400°F. for
1 hour *or* microwave on HIGH 10 1/2 to 12 1/2 minutes or until
fork-tender.

No-Fuss Potato Topper
*Top hot baked potatoes with PACE
Picante Sauce and shredded
Cheddar cheese.*

Mini Beef Loaves

PREP TIME: 15 MINUTES
COOK TIME: 30 MINUTES

1 can (10 1/4 ounces) FRANCO-AMERICAN Beef Gravy
1/2 cup PACE Picante Sauce
2 pounds ground beef
2 cups fresh bread crumbs
1 egg, beaten
6 cups hot mashed potatoes

1. Mix *1/4 cup* gravy, *1/4 cup* picante sauce, beef, bread crumbs and egg *thoroughly*. Shape *firmly* into 6 loaves and place in large baking pan.

2. Bake at 400°F. for 30 minutes or until no longer pink (160°F.).

3. In small saucepan mix remaining gravy and picante sauce. Heat through. Serve with meat loaves and potatoes. **Serves 6.**

Home-on-the-Range Supper

Meat Loaf with Roasted Garlic Potatoes (p.69)
Glazed Carrots
Avocado Melon Salad with Picante Honey Dressing (p.97)
Sourdough Rolls
Caramel Custard
Assorted Sodas

Meat Loaf with Roasted Garlic Potatoes

PREP TIME: 20 MINUTES
COOK TIME: 1 HOUR

1 cup PACE Picante Sauce
1 1/2 pounds ground beef
1 cup fresh bread crumbs
1 egg, beaten
2 tablespoons chopped fresh parsley *or* 2 teaspoons
   dried parsley flakes
1 tablespoon Worcestershire sauce
4 cloves garlic, minced *or* 1/2 teaspoon garlic powder
2 tablespoons vegetable oil
4 medium potatoes (about 1 1/4 pounds), *each* cut
   into 8 wedges
Paprika (optional)

1. Mix *1/2 cup* picante sauce, beef, bread crumbs, egg,
   parsley, Worcestershire and *2 cloves* garlic *thoroughly*.
   In large shallow-sided baking pan shape *firmly* into an
   8-by 4-inch loaf.

2. Mix oil and remaining garlic. Toss potatoes with oil mixture until evenly coated. Sprinkle with paprika, if desired.
   Place around meat loaf.

3. Bake at 350°F. for 1 hour or until meat loaf is no longer
   pink (160°F.). Pour remaining picante sauce over meat loaf
   before serving.
   Serves 6.

Family Spaghetti Pie

PREP TIME: 25 MINUTES
COOK TIME: 30 MINUTES
STAND TIME: 5 MINUTES

1 pound ground beef
1 cup PACE Picante Sauce
1 cup PREGO Spaghetti Sauce with Mushrooms
3 cups hot cooked spaghetti (about 6 ounces dry)
1/3 cup grated Parmesan cheese
1 egg, beaten
1 tablespoon margarine *or* butter, melted
1 cup ricotta cheese
1 cup shredded mozzarella cheese (4 ounces)
Fresh basil for garnish

1. In medium skillet over medium-high heat, cook beef until browned, stirring to separate meat. Pour off fat. Stir in picante sauce and spaghetti sauce. Heat through.

2. Mix spaghetti, Parmesan cheese, egg and margarine. Spread on bottom and up side of greased 10-inch pie plate. Spread ricotta cheese on spaghetti. Top with beef mixture.

3. Bake at 350°F. for 30 minutes or until hot. Sprinkle with mozzarella cheese. Let stand 5 minutes before serving. Cut into wedges. Serve with additional picante sauce and garnish with basil.
Serves 6.

Mexi-Corn Lasagna

PREP TIME: 20 MINUTES
COOK TIME: 30 MINUTES
STAND TIME: 10 MINUTES

1 container (16 ounces) cottage cheese
2 eggs, beaten
1/4 cup grated Parmesan cheese
1 teaspoon dried oregano leaves, crushed
1 pound ground beef
1 can (15 ounces) tomato sauce
1 cup PACE Picante Sauce
1 tablespoon chili powder
1 cup frozen whole kernel corn
12 corn tortillas (6-inch)
1 cup shredded Cheddar cheese (4 ounces)

1. Mix cottage cheese, eggs, Parmesan cheese and oregano. Set aside.

2. In medium skillet over medium-high heat, cook beef until browned, stirring to separate meat. Pour off fat. Stir in tomato sauce, picante sauce, chili powder and corn. Heat through.

3. Arrange *6* tortillas in bottom and up sides of 3-quart shallow baking dish. Top with *half* of the meat mixture and all the cheese mixture. Top with remaining *6* tortillas and remaining meat mixture.

4. Bake at 400°F. for 30 minutes or until hot. Sprinkle with Cheddar cheese. Let stand 10 minutes. Serve with additional picante sauce.
Serves 8.

Sloppy Joes

PREP TIME: 5 MINUTES
COOK TIME: 10 MINUTES

1 pound ground beef
3/4 cup PACE Picante Sauce
1/2 cup barbecue sauce
2 green onions, sliced (about 1/4 cup)
5 hamburger rolls, split and toasted

1. In medium skillet over medium-high heat, cook beef until browned, stirring to separate meat. Pour off fat.

2. Add picante sauce, barbecue sauce and onions. Reduce heat to low and heat through.

3. Divide meat mixture among rolls.
Makes 5 sandwiches.

White Gold

Salt was an absolute necessity in the Old West. Its abilities as a food preservative accounted for its cost—often four times greater than that of meat. Meat placed in oak barrels filled with brine would stay fresh for the entire trek by wagon train across the Rocky Mountains. In the fall, pioneer women would fill a barrel with alternating layers of salt and fresh eggs. This supply of eggs could last through the winter until the hens began to lay again in the spring.

Meatball Sandwiches

PREP TIME: 15 MINUTES
COOK TIME: 25 MINUTES

1 cup PACE Picante Sauce
1 pound ground beef
1 cup crushed tortilla chips
1 egg, beaten
1 tablespoon chopped fresh parsley *or* 1 teaspoon dried parsley flakes
1 1/2 cups PREGO Traditional Spaghetti Sauce
6 long hard rolls, split

1. Mix *1/2 cup* picante sauce, beef, chips, egg and parsley *thoroughly* and shape *firmly* into 18 (1 1/2-inch) meatballs.

2. In medium skillet mix spaghetti sauce and remaining picante sauce. Add meatballs. Over medium heat, heat to a boil. Reduce heat to low. Cover and cook 20 minutes or until meatballs are no longer pink, stirring occasionally.

3. Place meatballs and sauce in rolls.
Makes 6 sandwiches.

Chili Mac

PREP TIME: 10 MINUTES
COOK TIME: 25 MINUTES

1 pound ground beef
1 cup PACE Picante Sauce
1 tablespoon chili powder
1 can (14 1/2 ounces) whole peeled tomatoes, cut up
1 cup frozen whole kernel corn
3 cups cooked elbow macaroni (about 1 1/2 cups dry)
1/2 cup shredded Cheddar cheese (2 ounces)
Sliced avocado and sour cream for garnish

1. In medium skillet over medium-high heat, cook beef until browned, stirring to separate meat. Pour off fat.

2. Add picante sauce, chili powder, tomatoes and corn. Heat to a boil. Reduce heat to low. Cook 10 minutes. Add macaroni. Sprinkle cheese over macaroni mixture. Cover and heat until cheese is melted. Garnish with avocado and sour cream.
Serves 4.

An American Tradition: On average, an American spends $4.50 on ketchup and $7.43 on salsa—nearly double— each year.

Sloppy Joes (left, page 72) and Chili Mac (right, page 73).

Orange Picante Pork Chops

PREP TIME: 5 MINUTES
MARINATING TIME: 1 HOUR
COOK TIME: 15 MINUTES

3/4 cup PACE Picante Sauce
1/4 cup orange juice
1/4 teaspoon garlic powder *or* 2 cloves garlic, minced
4 boneless pork chops, 3/4 inch thick (about
1 pound), trimmed

1. Mix picante sauce, orange juice and garlic powder in shallow nonmetallic dish. Add chops and turn to coat. Cover and refrigerate 1 hour, turning chops occasionally.

2. Remove chops from marinade and place on lightly oiled grill rack over medium-hot coals. Grill uncovered 15 minutes or until chops are no longer pink, turning and brushing often with marinade. Discard remaining marinade. **Serves 4.**

Broiled Orange Picante Pork Chops: Prepare as in step 1. In step 2 remove chops from marinade and place on rack in broiler pan. Broil 4 inches from heat 15 minutes or until chops are no longer pink, turning and brushing often with marinade. Discard remaining marinade.

Nutritional Values Per Serving: Calories 191, Total Fat 8g, Saturated Fat 3g, Cholesterol 67mg, Sodium 389mg, Total Carbohydrate 5g, Dietary Fiber 1g, Protein 24g

Orange Beef and Peppers

PREP TIME: 15 MINUTES
COOK TIME: 25 MINUTES

**1 pound boneless beef sirloin *or* top round steak,
    3/4 inch thick**
2 tablespoons vegetable oil
**2 small red, yellow *or* green peppers, cut into strips
    (about 2 cups)**
1 large onion, sliced (about 1 cup)
1 jar (12 ounces) PEPPERIDGE FARM Beef Gravy
1/2 cup PACE Picante Sauce
1/4 cup orange juice
1 tablespoon soy sauce
1 teaspoon grated orange peel
4 cups hot cooked rice
Orange slice and fresh parsley for garnish

1. Slice beef into very thin strips.

2. In medium skillet over medium-high heat, heat *half* the oil.
   Add beef in 2 batches and stir-fry until browned. Set beef
   aside.

3. Reduce heat to medium. Add remaining oil. Add peppers
   and onion and stir-fry until tender-crisp.

4. Add gravy, picante sauce, orange juice, soy and orange
   peel. Heat to a boil. Return beef to pan and heat through.
   Serve over rice. Garnish with orange and parsley.
   Serves 4.

TIP: To make slicing easier, freeze beef 1 hour.

Casual Weekend Fiesta

Guacamole and Chips
Lasagna Roll-Ups (p.76)
Pepperidge Farm Garlic Bread
Antipasto Salad
Coffee Ice Cream with Cinnamon
Iced Tea and/or Iced Coffee

Lasagna Roll-Ups

PREP TIME: 30 MINUTES
COOK TIME: 35 MINUTES
STAND TIME: 10 MINUTES

1 cup ricotta cheese
1 can (about 4 ounces) mushroom stems and pieces, drained
1/2 cup refrigerated pesto sauce
8 lasagna noodles, cooked and drained
2 cups PREGO Traditional Spaghetti Sauce
3/4 cup PACE Picante Sauce
1 cup shredded mozzarella cheese (4 ounces)

1. Mix ricotta, mushrooms and pesto. Top each noodle with *1/4 cup* cheese mixture. Spread to edges. Roll up like a jelly roll. Place seam-side down in 2-quart shallow baking dish.

2. Mix spaghetti sauce and picante sauce and pour over roll-ups.

3. Bake at 400°F. for 30 minutes or until hot. Top with mozzarella cheese. Bake 5 minutes more or until cheese is melted. Let stand 10 minutes.
Serves 4.

Polenta Pie with Picante Sauce

PREP TIME: 30 MINUTES
CHILL TIME: 30 MINUTES
COOK TIME: 30 MINUTES

4 cups water
1 cup yellow cornmeal
1/2 cup grated Parmesan cheese
1 tablespoon vegetable oil
2 cups broccoli flowerets
1 1/2 cups sliced mushrooms (about 4 ounces)
1/8 teaspoon garlic powder *or* 1 clove garlic, minced
2 cups PREGO Traditional Spaghetti Sauce
3/4 cup PACE Picante Sauce

1. To make polenta, in large saucepan over medium-high heat, heat water to a boil. Gradually whisk in cornmeal. Reduce heat to low. Cook 20 minutes, stirring often. Stir in cheese. Cook until thickened. Pour into 9-inch round baking pan. Cover and freeze 20 to 30 minutes or until firm. (Or, cover and refrigerate polenta 4 hours or until firm.)

2. In medium skillet over medium heat, heat oil. Add broccoli, mushrooms and garlic powder and cook until tender-crisp. Add spaghetti sauce and picante sauce.

3. Cut polenta into 4 wedges. Arrange in 3-quart shallow baking dish. Pour vegetable mixture over wedges. Bake at 400°F. for 30 minutes. If desired, serve with additional cheese.
Serves 4.

Polenta Pie with Picante Sauce (top, page 77)
and Lasagna Roll-Ups (bottom, page 76).

Sizzlers From The Grill

Chicken with Picante Peach Salsa

PREP TIME: 15 MINUTES
COOK TIME: 15 MINUTES

2/3 cup PACE Picante Sauce
2 tablespoons lime juice
1 can (about 15 ounces) peach halves in heavy syrup,
    drained and diced
1/3 cup chopped green *or* red pepper
2 green onions, sliced (about 1/4 cup)
1/2 teaspoon ground cumin
1/2 teaspoon chili powder
6 skinless, boneless chicken breast halves
    (about 1 1/2 pounds)
1/2 cup peach *or* apricot preserves

1. For salsa, mix *1/3 cup* picante sauce, lime juice, peaches,
   pepper and onions. Set aside.

2. Mix cumin and chili powder. Sprinkle both sides of
   chicken with cumin mixture. Mix remaining picante
   sauce and preserves.

3. Place chicken on lightly oiled grill rack over medium-hot
   coals. Grill uncovered 15 minutes or until chicken is no
   longer pink, turning and brushing often with preserve
   mixture. Discard remaining preserve mixture.
   Serve chicken with peach salsa.
   Serves 6.

Nutritional Values Per Serving: Calories 241, Total Fat 3g, Saturated
Fat 1g, Cholesterol 73mg, Sodium 273mg, Total Carbohydrate 26g,
Dietary Fiber 1g, Protein 27g

Chicken with Picante Peach Salsa (left, page 79) and
Marinated Beef Steak (right, page 84).

▲▲▲▲▲▲▲▲▲▲▲▲▲▲▲▲▲

Where There's Smoke...

*Grilling, smoking and barbe-
cuing are all rooted in the
fact that earliest man liked
his meat cooked and that
wood was the fuel at hand.
In the Old West, Dutch and
German settlers brought their
designs for smokehouses with
them. Hams, bacon, birds
and large pieces of meat were
cooked for long periods in
sealed spaces over low heat.
This made for a thorough
cooking and smoky taste.
Grilling over an
open fire on the
trail produced food
that was crispy out-
side and moist inside.
Seems like the best things in
life never change.*

▼▼▼▼▼▼▼▼▼▼▼▼▼▼▼▼

At Root, It's Wood

If you use charcoal briquettes, it's easy and painless to grill. Using hardwood, however, lets you add something extra to the food. Experts say they can tell the wood used by the taste of the food.

- *A strong heavy bacon-like flavor is probably hickory.*
- *Maple adds a smoky, mellow, slightly sweet flavor to food.*
- *Mesquite and oak add a taste of honey.*

Old Southwest Barbecue

Bean and Cheese Quesadillas (p.18)
Simply Spicy Grilled Chicken (p.80)
Spicy Onion Burgers (p.84)
Baked Beans
Coleslaw
Sliced Watermelon
Minted Iced Tea

Simply Spicy Grilled Chicken

PREP TIME: 5 MINUTES
COOK TIME: 40 MINUTES

3/4 cup PACE Picante Sauce
3/4 cup barbecue sauce
2 pounds chicken parts, skin removed
1 cup uncooked regular long-grain white rice
2 green onions, sliced (about 1/4 cup)
Orange slices and fresh thyme for garnish

1. Mix picante sauce and barbecue sauce. Reserve *3/4 cup* and set aside.

2. Place chicken on lightly oiled grill rack over medium-hot coals. Grill uncovered 20 minutes, turning often. Brush with remaining picante sauce mixture and grill 20 minutes more or until chicken is no longer pink, turning and brushing often with picante sauce mixture. Discard remaining picante sauce mixture.

3. Cook rice according to package directions without salt. Stir in reserved picante sauce mixture and onions. Serve with chicken. Garnish with orange slices and thyme.
Serves 4.

 Nutritional Values Per Serving: Calories 385, Total Fat 7g, Saturated Fat 2g, Cholesterol 82mg, Sodium 801mg, Total Carbohydrate 48g, Dietary Fiber 3g, Protein 32g

Grilled Chicken Tacos

PREP TIME: 15 MINUTES
COOK TIME: 15 MINUTES

1/2 cup PACE Picante Sauce
2 teaspoons lemon juice
2 medium avocados, peeled, pitted and diced
1 medium tomato, chopped (about 1 cup)
2 green onions, sliced (about 1/4 cup)
6 skinless, boneless chicken breast halves
    (about 1 1/2 pounds)
2 tablespoons vegetable oil
12 flour tortillas (8-inch)
3/4 cup shredded Cheddar cheese (3 ounces)
Fresh cilantro for garnish

1. Mix picante sauce, lemon juice, avocados, tomato and onions. Set aside.

2. Brush chicken with oil. Place chicken on lightly oiled grill rack over medium-hot coals. Grill uncovered 15 minutes or until chicken is no longer pink, turning once.

3. Warm tortillas according to package directions. Slice chicken into thin strips and place down center of each tortilla. Top with avocado mixture and cheese. Roll up. Serve with additional picante sauce. Garnish with cilantro.
Serves 6.

Grilled Chicken Tacos (top, page 81)
and Simply Spicy Grilled Chicken (bottom, page 80).

Garlic Grilled Chicken

PREP TIME: 15 MINUTES
COOK TIME: 10 MINUTES

1 pound skinless, boneless chicken breasts
3/4 cup PACE Picante Sauce
1 tablespoon vegetable oil
1 tablespoon lime juice
1/4 teaspoon garlic powder *or* 2 cloves garlic, minced
1/2 teaspoon ground cumin

1. Place chicken between 2 pieces of plastic wrap. With meat mallet or rolling pin, pound chicken to 1/2-inch thickness. Cut lengthwise into 1-inch-wide strips.

2. Mix picante sauce, oil, lime juice, garlic powder and cumin. Add chicken and toss to coat.

3. On 8 long skewers, thread chicken accordion-style. Reserve picante sauce mixture. Place skewers on lightly oiled grill rack over medium-hot coals. Grill uncovered 10 minutes or until chicken is no longer pink, turning and brushing often with reserved picante sauce mixture. Discard remaining picante sauce mixture.
Serves 4.

 Nutritional Values Per Serving: Calories 188, Total Fat 7g, Saturated Fat 1g, Cholesterol 72mg, Sodium 397mg, Total Carbohydrate 4g, Dietary Fiber 1g, Protein 27g

Grilled Vegetable Sandwiches

PREP TIME: 15 MINUTES
COOK TIME: 15 MINUTES

1/2 cup PACE Picante Sauce
1/4 cup red wine vinegar
1 teaspoon dried oregano leaves, crushed
1/4 teaspoon garlic powder *or* 2 cloves garlic, minced
2 portobello mushrooms (about 4 ounces)
1 small eggplant (about 10 ounces), sliced lengthwise
   1/2 inch thick
2 small zucchini, sliced in half lengthwise
1 large green *or* red pepper, cut into quarters
4 long sandwich rolls, split and toasted
1/2 cup shredded mozzarella cheese (2 ounces)

1. Mix picante sauce, vinegar, oregano and garlic powder.

2. Place mushrooms, eggplant, zucchini and pepper on
   lightly oiled grill rack over medium-hot coals. Grill
   uncovered 15 minutes or until vegetables are tender,
   turning and brushing often with picante sauce mixture.
   Slice mushrooms, zucchini and pepper.

3. Arrange vegetables in rolls. Top with cheese. Serve with
   additional picante sauce.
   Makes 4 sandwiches.

TIP: To toast rolls, place cut-side down on grill.

Spicy Onion Burgers

PREP TIME: 10 MINUTES
COOK TIME: 10 MINUTES

1 1/2 pounds ground beef
1/2 cup PACE Picante Sauce
1 pouch CAMPBELL'S Dry Onion Soup and Recipe Mix
Lettuce leaves
Tomato slices
6 hamburger rolls, split
Avocado slices

1. Mix beef, picante sauce and soup mix *thoroughly.* Shape *firmly* into 6 patties, 1/2 inch thick.

2. Place patties on lightly oiled grill rack over medium-hot coals. Grill 10 minutes or until no longer pink (160°F.), turning once.

3. Place lettuce, tomato and patties on 6 roll halves. Top with avocado, additional picante sauce and remaining roll halves.
Makes 6 sandwiches.

Sizzling Toppers.
Top hamburgers and
frankfurters with PACE
Picante Sauce.

Marinated Beef Steak   *Pace*

PREP TIME: 10 MINUTES
MARINATING TIME: 30 MINUTES
COOK TIME: 25 MINUTES

2/3 cup PACE Picante Sauce
1/3 cup vegetable oil
1 teaspoon dried oregano leaves, crushed
1/4 teaspoon garlic powder *or* 2 cloves garlic, minced
1 1/2 pounds beef top round steak, 1 1/2 inches thick

1. Mix picante sauce, oil, oregano and garlic powder in large shallow nonmetallic dish. Add steak and turn to coat. Cover and refrigerate 30 minutes, turning steak occasionally.

2. Remove steak from marinade and place on lightly oiled grill rack over medium-hot coals. Grill uncovered to desired doneness (allow 25 minutes for medium), turning once and brushing often with marinade. Thinly slice steak. Discard remaining marinade.

3. Serve with additional picante sauce.
Serves 6.

Grilled Skewered Shrimp

PREP TIME: 20 MINUTES
COOK TIME: 10 MINUTES

2/3 cup PACE Picante Sauce
1 can (8 ounces) tomato sauce
3 tablespoons packed brown sugar
2 tablespoons lemon juice
1 1/2 pounds large shrimp, peeled and deveined

1. Mix picante sauce, tomato sauce, sugar and lemon juice. Add shrimp and toss to coat.

2. On 12 long skewers, thread shrimp. Reserve picante sauce mixture.

3. Place skewers on lightly oiled grill rack over medium-hot coals. Grill uncovered 10 minutes or until shrimp turn pink, turning and brushing often with reserved picante sauce mixture. Discard remaining picante sauce mixture. **Serves 6.**

 Nutritional Values Per Serving: Calories 124, Total Fat 1g, Saturated Fat 0g, Cholesterol 149mg, Sodium 621mg, Total Carbohydrate 12g, Dietary Fiber 1g, Protein 17g

Easy Picante Basting Sauce
Combine PACE Picante Sauce, lime juice and garlic. Use as a basting sauce for shrimp while grilling or broiling.

Grilled Skewered Shrimp (left, page 85)
and Spicy Onion Burgers (right, page 84).

Grilled Pork in Pita

PREP TIME: 10 MINUTES
COOK TIME: 15 MINUTES

3/4 cup PACE Picante Sauce
1/2 cup plain yogurt
1 teaspoon lime juice
1/4 teaspoon garlic powder *or* 2 cloves garlic, minced
4 boneless pork chops, 3/4 inch thick (about
** 1 pound), trimmed**
6 pita breads (6-inch), warmed
1 cup shredded lettuce
1 green onion, sliced (about 2 tablespoons)

1. Mix *3 tablespoons* picante sauce, yogurt and lime juice. Cover and refrigerate.

2. Mix remaining picante sauce and garlic powder. Place chops on lightly oiled grill rack over medium-hot coals. Grill uncovered 15 minutes or until chops are no longer pink, turning and brushing often with picante sauce mixture. Discard remaining picante sauce mixture.

3. Slice pork into thin strips and place down center of each pita. Top with yogurt sauce, lettuce and onion. Fold pita around filling.
Serves 6.

TIP: To warm pita breads, wrap in a plain paper towel. Microwave on HIGH 1 minute or until warm.

 Nutritional Values Per Serving: Calories 242, Total Fat 6g, Saturated Fat 2g, Cholesterol 47mg, Sodium 473mg, Total Carbohydrate 25g, Dietary Fiber 1g, Protein 20g

Grilled Swordfish Steaks with Citrus Salsa

PREP TIME: 15 MINUTES
COOK TIME: 10 MINUTES

3/4 cup PACE Picante Sauce
1 teaspoon grated orange peel
2 tablespoons orange juice
1 tablespoon chopped fresh cilantro
1 cup coarsely chopped oranges
1 medium tomato, chopped (about 1 cup)
2 green onions, sliced (about 1/4 cup)
4 swordfish steaks, 1 inch thick (about 1 1/2 pounds)

1. Mix picante sauce, orange peel, orange juice and cilantro. Reserve *1/2 cup*. For salsa, add oranges, tomato and onions to remaining picante sauce mixture. Set aside.

2. Place swordfish on lightly oiled grill rack over medium-hot coals. Grill uncovered 10 minutes or until fish flakes easily when tested with a fork, turning once and brushing often with reserved picante sauce mixture. Discard remaining picante sauce mixture.

3. Serve fish with orange salsa.
   Serves 4.

Nutritional Values Per Serving: Calories 246, Total Fat 6g, Saturated Fat 2g, Cholesterol 61mg, Sodium 480mg, Total Carbohydrate 13g, Dietary Fiber 3g, Protein 32g.

Brunch, Egg & Cheese Dishes

Cream Cheese and Mushroom Enchiladas

PREP TIME: 20 MINUTES
COOK TIME: 35 MINUTES

1 cup PACE Picante Sauce
1 can (14 1/2 ounces) whole peeled tomatoes, cut up
1 tablespoon vegetable oil
4 cups sliced mushrooms (about 12 ounces)
1/8 teaspoon garlic powder *or* 1 clove garlic, minced
1 package (8 ounces) cream cheese, cubed
8 flour tortillas (6-inch)
3/4 cup shredded Monterey Jack cheese (3 ounces)
Sliced green onions

1. In medium saucepan mix picante sauce and tomatoes. Over medium heat, heat to a boil. Reduce heat to low and cook 5 minutes.

2. In medium skillet over medium heat, heat oil. Add mushrooms and garlic powder and cook until liquid has evaporated. Remove from heat. Add cream cheese and stir until melted.

3. Spoon about *1/4 cup* mushroom mixture down center of each tortilla. Roll up and place seam-side down in 2-quart shallow baking dish.

4. Spoon picante sauce mixture over enchiladas. Cover and bake at 350°F. for 30 minutes or until hot. Uncover. Top with cheese. Bake 5 minutes more or until cheese is melted. Sprinkle with onions.
Serves 4.

Huevos Rancheros (left, page 90) and Cream Cheese and Mushroom Enchiladas (right, page 89).

How Hot?

What makes a pepper "hot"? Capsaicin. And the amount of capsaicin in any pepper can be measured in Scoville Units. That's the number of units of water it takes to wipe out the heat from a unit of pepper. While a sweet Bell Pepper has a Scoville Unit rating of zero, it can take up to 300,000 units of water to neutralize the heat from one unit of a Scotch Bonnet—the hottest pepper known to man. Jalapeño peppers—which give PACE its texture as well as taste—can come in a range of heat levels from no-heat (a recent innovation of PACE's pepper experts) to a high of 5,000 Scoville Units.

Huevos Rancheros

PREP TIME: 10 MINUTES
COOK TIME: 15 MINUTES

1/2 cup PACE Picante Sauce
1 teaspoon chili powder
1 can (14 1/2 ounces) whole peeled tomatoes, cut up
4 flour tortillas (8-inch)
1 tablespoon margarine *or* butter
8 eggs
Fresh parsley for garnish

1. In medium saucepan mix picante sauce, chili powder and tomatoes. Over medium heat, heat through.

2. Warm tortillas according to package directions.

3. In medium skillet over medium heat, heat margarine. Add eggs in 2 batches and cook to desired doneness. Arrange 2 eggs on each tortilla. Top with picante sauce mixture. Garnish with parsley.
Serves 4.

Alternative Fuel: *Race car driver A.J. Foyt has been known to bring PACE sauces to help fuel his food during the Indy 500.*

Potato Frittata Olé

PREP TIME: 20 MINUTES
COOK TIME: 25 MINUTES

1/4 cup margarine *or* butter
4 cups frozen hash brown potatoes (about 1 pound)
1 1/2 cups sliced mushrooms (about 4 ounces)
2 green onions, chopped (about 1/4 cup)
1 teaspoon dried basil leaves, crushed *or* 1 tablespoon chopped fresh basil leaves
8 eggs, beaten
1 cup PACE Picante Sauce
1 cup shredded Cheddar cheese (4 ounces)

1. In medium oven-safe skillet over medium heat, heat margarine. Add potatoes, mushrooms, onions and basil. Cover and cook 10 minutes or until potatoes are tender, stirring occasionally.

2. Pour eggs into pan. Bake at 350°F. for 20 minutes or until knife inserted near center comes out clean.

3. Top with picante sauce and cheese. Bake 5 minutes more or until cheese is melted. Cut into wedges.
Serves 6.

TIP: To make skillet oven-safe, cover handle with foil.

Quick Quesadillas

PREP TIME: 15 MINUTES
COOK TIME: 20 MINUTES

6 flour tortillas (8-inch)
1 1/2 cups shredded Monterey Jack cheese (6 ounces)
2 green onions, sliced (about 1/4 cup)
3/4 cup PACE Picante Sauce
1 tablespoon margarine *or* butter, melted
1 medium tomato, chopped (about 1 cup)

1. Top half of each tortilla with cheese, onions and *1 table-spoon* picante sauce. Moisten edges of tortillas with water. Fold over and press edges together. Place on 2 baking sheets. Brush with margarine.

2. Bake at 400°F. for 20 minutes or until golden.

3. Mix remaining picante sauce and tomato. Serve with quesadillas.
   Makes 6 quesadillas.

TIP: To melt margarine, remove wrapper and place in microwave-safe cup. Cover and microwave on HIGH 30 seconds.

Potato Frittata Olé (top, page 90)
and Quick Quesadillas (bottom, page 91).

Breakfast Tacos

PREP TIME: 15 MINUTES
COOK TIME: 10 MINUTES

1 tablespoon margarine *or* butter
1 medium potato, cooked and diced (about 1 cup)
4 eggs, beaten
4 slices bacon, cooked and crumbled
4 flour tortillas (8-inch)
3/4 cup shredded Cheddar cheese (3 ounces)
1/2 cup PACE Picante Sauce

1. In medium skillet over medium heat, heat margarine. Add potato and cook until lightly browned. Add eggs and bacon. Cook until set but still moist.

2. Warm tortillas according to package directions. Spoon about *1/2 cup* potato mixture down center of each tortilla. Top with cheese and picante sauce. Roll up.
Makes 4 tacos.

Picante Sunrise
Mix PACE Picante Sauce and your favorite vegetables into the egg mixture for a zesty omelet.

Picante Brunch Quiche

PREP TIME: 10 MINUTES
COOK TIME: 35 MINUTES
STAND TIME: 10 MINUTES

1 cup shredded Cheddar cheese (4 ounces)
4 slices bacon, cooked and crumbled
2 green onions, sliced (about 1/4 cup)
1 (9-inch) frozen pie crust
3 eggs, beaten
1/2 cup PACE Picante Sauce
1/2 cup half-and-half *or* milk

1. Preheat oven to 375°F.

2. Arrange cheese, bacon and onions in pie crust. Mix eggs, picante sauce and half-and-half. Pour over cheese mixture.

3. Bake 35 minutes or until crust is golden and knife inserted in center comes out clean. Let stand 10 minutes. Serve with additional picante sauce.
Serves 6.

Unsung Heroes

At the turn of the century, approximately one-fifth of America's cowboys were African-Americans. The most famous of these was Nat Love (1854-1921). A trail driver, rodeo champion, Indian fighter and crack shot—he wrote a biography in 1907 that not only sold like wildfire, it read like it as well. There were real cowgirls, too. Martha "Calamity Jane" Cannary (1852-1903) was perhaps the most famous— known for wearing men's clothes, swearing, drinking and packing a pistol which she was absolutely willing to use.

Cornbread Squares

PREP TIME: 10 MINUTES
COOK TIME: 20 MINUTES

1 package (7 1/2 to 8 1/2 ounces) corn muffin mix
1/2 cup PACE Picante Sauce
1/2 cup shredded Cheddar cheese (2 ounces)

1. Preheat oven to 400°F. Grease 8-inch square baking pan.

2. Prepare corn muffin mix according to package directions. Spread *half* the batter in pan. Top with picante sauce and cheese. Spread remaining batter over cheese.

3. Bake 20 to 25 minutes or until toothpick inserted in center comes out clean. Cut into squares.
Serves 9.

Ranch-Style Bonanza Brunch

Assorted Fruit Juices
Scrambled Tortilla Eggs (p.95)
Cornbread Squares (p.94)
Picante Brunch Quiche (p.93)
Crisp Bacon and Ham
Fresh Melon and Berries
Coffee and Tea

Scrambled Tortilla Eggs *Pace*

PREP TIME: 10 MINUTES
COOK TIME: 15 MINUTES

8 eggs, beaten
1 cup PACE Picante Sauce
2 tablespoons margarine *or* butter
1 cup shredded Monterey Jack cheese (4 ounces)
1 cup crumbled tortilla chips
1 large avocado, peeled, pitted and sliced

1. Mix eggs and *2 tablespoons* picante sauce.

2. In medium skillet over medium heat, heat margarine. Pour in egg mixture. As eggs begin to set, stir lightly so uncooked egg mixture flows to bottom. Cook until set but still moist. Stir in cheese and chips.

3. In small saucepan heat remaining picante sauce. Spoon over eggs. Top with avocado. Serve immediately. **Serves 4.**

Easy San Antonio-Style Eggs
Top fried or scrambled eggs with PACE Picante Sauce.

Cornbread Squares (top, page 94) and Scrambled Tortilla Eggs (bottom, page 95).

Salads & Sides

Avocado Melon Salad with Picante Honey Dressing

PREP TIME: 20 MINUTES

1/2 cup PACE Picante Sauce
3 tablespoons honey
2 tablespoons lime juice
1 tablespoon vegetable oil
3 cups spinach leaves torn in bite-size pieces
2 cups cantaloupe cut in cubes
1 large avocado, peeled, pitted and cut into cubes
1/4 cup toasted slivered almonds

1. In small bowl mix picante sauce, honey, lime juice and oil.

2. In large bowl toss spinach, cantaloupe, avocado and picante mixture until evenly coated. Sprinkle with almonds. Serve immediately.
   Serves 6.

TIP: To toast almonds, arrange almonds in single layer in shallow-sided baking pan. Bake at 350°F. for 10 minutes or until lightly browned.

Slimming Substitutes

PACE picante sauces have only 5 calories per tablespoon and are naturally fat free. Compare that with a tablespoon of mayonnaise or butter which weigh in at about 100 calories per tablespoon and 11 grams of fat. Simply using two flavorful tablespoons of PACE picante sauce instead of regular Italian salad dressing can cut as much as 120 calories and about 14 grams of fat.

Avocado Melon Salad with Picante Honey Dressing (left, page 97) and Spanish-Style Rice (right, page 98).

Spanish-Style Rice

PREP TIME: 5 MINUTES
COOK TIME: 30 MINUTES

1 tablespoon vegetable oil
1 cup uncooked regular long-grain white rice
1 can (10 1/2 ounces) CAMPBELL'S condensed
   Chicken Broth
1 cup water
1/2 cup PACE Picante Sauce
1/2 teaspoon ground cumin
1/4 teaspoon garlic powder *or* 2 cloves garlic, minced
1 medium tomato, chopped (about 1 cup)
1 cup frozen peas

1. In medium skillet over medium heat, heat oil. Add rice
and cook until browned, stirring constantly.

2. Stir in broth, water, picante sauce, cumin and garlic
powder. Heat to boil. Reduce heat to low. Cover and cook
15 minutes. Add tomato and peas and cook 5 minutes more
or until rice is done and most of liquid is absorbed.
Serves 4.

California Chicken Salad Tacos

PREP TIME: 20 MINUTES

3/4 cup PACE Picante Sauce
2 tablespoons lime juice
1/2 teaspoon chili powder
2 cups cooked chicken strips
3 cups shredded lettuce
12 flour tortillas (8-inch)
1 medium tomato, chopped (about 1 cup)
1 cup shredded Cheddar cheese (4 ounces)

1. In large bowl mix picante sauce, lime juice and chili powder.
Add chicken and lettuce and toss until evenly coated.

2. Spoon about *1/2 cup* chicken mixture down center of each
tortilla. Top with tomato, cheese and additional picante
sauce. Roll up.
Makes 12 tacos.

Backyard Summer Buffet Olé

Grilled Chicken Salad (p.99)
Seven-Layer Meatless Tortilla Pie (p.49)
Chilled Rice Salad
Sliced Tomatoes with Cilantro and Olive Oil
Fresh Fruit Tart
Iced Tea and/or Sangria Punch

Grilled Chicken Salad

PREP TIME: 10 MINUTES
COOK TIME: 15 MINUTES

1 cup PACE Picante Sauce
3 tablespoons vegetable oil
1 tablespoon lime juice
1/4 teaspoon garlic powder *or* 2 cloves garlic, minced
**4 skinless, boneless chicken breast halves (about
    1 pound)**
1/2 teaspoon chili powder
6 cups salad greens torn in bite-size pieces
**1 can (about 16 ounces) black beans, rinsed
    and drained**
2 medium oranges, peeled and sliced
2 green onions, sliced (about 1/4 cup)

1. In small bowl mix picante sauce, *2 tablespoons* oil, lime juice
   and garlic powder. Set aside.

2. Sprinkle both sides of chicken with chili powder. Brush with
   remaining oil. Place chicken on lightly oiled grill rack over
   medium-hot coals. Grill uncovered 15 minutes or until chick-
   en is no longer pink, turning once. Slice chicken into strips.

3. Arrange salad greens on 4 plates. Arrange chicken, beans
   and oranges over salad greens. Sprinkle with onions and
   pour picante sauce mixture over salads.
   Serves 4.

*California Chicken Salad Tacos (top, page 98)
and Grilled Chicken Salad (bottom, page 99).*

San Antonio Shrimp 'n' Shells Salad

PREP TIME: 25 MINUTES
CHILL TIME: 2 HOURS

2/3 cup PACE Picante Sauce
1/3 cup mayonnaise
1/4 cup chopped fresh cilantro
3/4 teaspoon ground cumin
2 1/2 cups cooked medium shell macaroni
   (about 2 cups dry)
1 medium green pepper, cut into 2-inch-long strips
   (about 1 1/2 cups)
2 green onions, sliced (about 1/4 cup)
1 pound medium shrimp, cooked, peeled and
   deveined
1 1/2 cups cherry tomatoes cut in half

1. In small bowl mix picante sauce, mayonnaise, cilantro and
   cumin.

2. In large bowl toss macaroni, pepper, onions, shrimp and
   picante sauce mixture until evenly coated. Refrigerate at
   least 2 hours. Stir in tomatoes.
   Serves 6.

Highest Acclaim: Declaring that PACE belongs on top of everything except ice cream, members of a U.S. mountain climbing team carried a jar to the top of Mount Everest in 1985.

Stir-Fried Beef Salad in Tortilla Cups

PREP TIME: 20 MINUTES
COOK TIME: 15 MINUTES

4 flour tortillas (8-inch)
1 pound boneless beef sirloin *or* top round steak,
 3/4 inch thick
1/4 teaspoon garlic powder *or* 2 cloves garlic, minced
1/4 teaspoon salt
1 tablespoon vegetable oil
1/2 cup PACE Picante Sauce
1/4 cup prepared Italian salad dressing
4 green onions, cut into 1-inch pieces (about 1 cup)
1 cup cherry tomatoes cut in half
4 cups salad greens torn in bite-size pieces

1. Preheat oven to 400°F. In shallow-sided baking pan place four 4-ounce custard cups, upside down. Soften tortillas according to package directions. Drape 1 tortilla over each cup. Bake 10 minutes or until edges are golden. Remove from cups and cool.

2. Slice beef into very thin strips. Toss beef with garlic powder and salt.

3. In medium skillet over medium-high heat, heat oil. Add beef mixture in 2 batches and stir-fry until browned. Set aside.

4. Add picante sauce, dressing, onions and tomatoes. Heat to a boil. Return beef to pan and heat through.

5. Arrange 1 cup salad greens in each tortilla cup. Spoon meat mixture over salad greens.
 Serves 4.

BLT Salad Toss

PREP TIME: 20 MINUTES

1/2 cup PACE Picante Sauce
1/4 cup prepared Italian salad dressing
6 cups romaine lettuce torn in bite-size pieces
2 medium tomatoes, cut into thin wedges
2/3 cup sliced pitted ripe olives
2 cups corn chips
1/2 cup shredded Cheddar cheese (2 ounces)
3 slices bacon, cooked and crumbled

1. In small bowl mix picante sauce and dressing.

2. In large bowl toss lettuce, tomatoes, olives, chips and picante sauce mixture until evenly coated. Top with cheese and bacon. Serve immediately.
Serves 6.

Cheesy Garlic Potatoes

PREP TIME: 10 MINUTES
COOK TIME: 10 MINUTES

1 can (10 3/4 ounces) CAMPBELL'S condensed
  Cheddar Cheese Soup
1/2 cup PACE Picante Sauce
1 teaspoon garlic powder
4 cups cubed cooked potatoes (about 4 medium)
Paprika
2 tablespoons chopped fresh cilantro

In medium skillet mix soup, picante sauce and garlic powder. Add potatoes. Over medium heat, heat through, stirring often. Sprinkle with paprika and cilantro. Serve with additional picante sauce.
Serves 6 to 8.

Texas Tailgate Party

Fiesta Tortilla Roll-Ups (p.19)
Assorted Hoagies
Best-of-the-West Bean Salad (p.103)
**San Antonio Shrimp 'n' Shells Salad
(p.100)**
Chocolate Cake
Assorted Sodas and/or Mexican Beers

President's Pick: PACE was the featured Picante Sauce at the 1988 Presidential Inauguration.

Best-of-the-West Bean Salad

PREP TIME: 10 MINUTES
CHILL TIME: 2 HOURS

3/4 cup PACE Picante Sauce
2 tablespoons chopped fresh cilantro
2 tablespoons red wine vinegar
1 tablespoon vegetable oil
1 large green pepper, diced (about 1 1/3 cups)
1 medium red onion, very thinly sliced (about 1/2 cup)
**1 can (about 15 ounces) kidney beans, rinsed and
    drained**
**1 can (about 15 ounces) pinto beans, rinsed and
    drained**

Mix picante sauce, cilantro, vinegar, oil, pepper, onion, kidney
beans and pinto beans. Refrigerate at least 2 hours, stirring
occasionally. Garnish with additional cilantro.
Serves 8.

Nutritional Values Per Serving: Calories 144, Total Fat 2g,
Saturated Fat 0g, Cholesterol 0mg, Sodium 361mg,
Total Carbohydrate 24g, Dietary Fiber 1g, Protein 8g

Best-of-the-West Bean Salad (left, page 103)
and Cheesy Garlic Potatoes (right, page 102).

Thai Chicken Fettuccine Salad

PREP TIME: 25 MINUTES
COOK TIME: 5 MINUTES

1 cup PACE Picante Sauce
1/4 cup chunky peanut butter
2 tablespoons honey
2 tablespoons orange juice
1 teaspoon soy sauce
1/2 teaspoon ground ginger
3 cups cooked fettuccine (about 6 ounces dry)
2 cups cubed cooked chicken
Salad greens
Chopped red pepper and chopped fresh cilantro
for garnish

1. In medium skillet mix picante sauce, peanut butter, honey, orange juice, soy and ginger. Over low heat, heat through, stirring constantly.

2. Add fettuccine and chicken. Toss mixture until evenly coated. Serve on salad greens. Garnish with red pepper and cilantro.
Serves 4.

Layered Tex-Mex Salad

PREP TIME: 20 MINUTES

1/2 cup PACE Picante Sauce
1/2 cup mayonnaise
1/4 cup sour cream or plain yogurt
3 cups coarsely shredded lettuce
2 medium tomatoes, chopped (about 2 cups)
1 small cucumber, cut in half lengthwise and sliced
  (about 1 1/2 cups)
1 medium red onion, sliced (about 1/2 cup)
1 large avocado, peeled, pitted and thinly sliced
1/4 cup sliced pitted ripe olives

1. In small bowl mix picante sauce, mayonnaise and sour
   cream.

2. In large clear glass bowl layer lettuce, tomatoes, cucumber,
   onion and avocado. Spoon picante sauce mixture over
   salad mixture. Sprinkle with olives. Serve immediately.
   Serves 8.

Too Much Of A Good Thing?

It hardly seems possible, but even the fiercest hot pepper lover can find those jalapeños doing a number on the mouth. The absolutely worst thing to put out a jalapeño fire is water. Water actually makes matters worse by spreading the hot oil around the mouth. Reach instead for milk, bread or a lemon slice. Milk helps dissolve the hot oils. Bread absorbs them. A lemon both cuts the oil and cools the mouth.

Picante Pinto Beans with Bacon

PREP TIME: 10 MINUTES
COOK TIME: 10 MINUTES

1 cup PACE Picante Sauce
1/4 cup ketchup *or* barbecue sauce
1/4 cup packed brown sugar
1 teaspoon ground cumin
4 slices bacon, cooked and crumbled
2 cans (about 15 ounces *each*) pinto beans, drained
Sliced jalapeño for garnish

In medium saucepan mix picante sauce, ketchup, sugar, cumin, bacon and beans. Over medium heat, heat through. Garnish with jalapeño.
Serves 6.

Easy Southern Sides
Spicy Rice
Stir a few tablespoons PACE Picante Sauce into cooked rice.

Tex-Mex Beans
Add PACE Picante Sauce to pinto beans or pork and beans while heating.

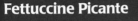 ## Fettuccine Picante

PREP TIME: 20 MINUTES
COOK TIME: 5 MINUTES

1/2 cup PACE Picante Sauce
1/2 cup sour cream
1/3 cup grated Parmesan cheese
4 cups hot cooked fettuccine (about 8 ounces dry)
2 tablespoons chopped fresh cilantro

In large saucepan mix picante sauce, sour cream and cheese. Over medium heat, heat through. Toss with fettuccine and cilantro. Serve with additional picante sauce and cilantro. Serves 4.

South-of-the-Border Patio Party

Grilled Shrimp
Fettuccine Picante (p.107)
Steamed Broccoli and Cauliflower
Cornbread
Sorbet with Assorted
Pepperidge Farm Cookies
Iced Tea and/or Margaritas

Picante Pinto Beans with Bacon (top, page 106) and Fettuccine Picante (bottom, page 107).

Index

Index

Index

Pace 50th Anniversary Cookbook

Since 1947 in San Antonio, Pace has been putting up its bold and spicy picante sauce. Pace is real proud of its down-home flavor, and each year more and more people seem to be enjoying this authentic taste of Texas. Now, with the *Pace Family Recipe Round-Up* cookbook they've corralled 50 years of great-tasting recipes to share with your family and friends. Inside you'll find appetizers, chilies and stews, Southwest main dishes and everyday family favorites, sizzlers from the grill, and more! Full-color photographs are included for almost every recipe, and symbols indicating "bold and spicy," "contest winner," "classic Pace recipe," "low fat," and "ready in 30 minutes or less" are given with the recipes. Lots of lively cowboy lore and fun facts are included throughout the book—perfect to share around the campfire!

Hardcover, wire-o book: 9x7 inches, 112 pages, 72 color recipe photographs, 100 recipes. Price $9.95 each; includes postage and handling.

Swanson® Broth Easy Low-Fat Recipes

Inside the *Swanson Broth Easy Low-Fat Recipes* cookbook there are over 60 recipes that will inspire you to enjoy low-fat cooking every day—quick skillet dishes, one-dish casseroles, speedy stir-fries, plus salads, pasta, vegetables, and more. With the many varieties of Swanson Broth, you'll discover how broth adds full flavor to your favorite dishes without adding extra fat. And, with more than 40 mouth-watering color photographs, you'll see how delicious low-fat cooking can be. Featured are consumer tips on using Swanson Broth in low-fat cooking, plus dozens of nutritional tips throughout the book.

Hardcover book: 8x8 inches, 96 pages, 43 color recipe photographs, 67 recipes. Price $6.50 each; includes postage and handling.

Campbell's® Back Label Recipes

With *Campbell's Back Label Recipes and more!* cookbook, you'll own a collection of your favorite recipes that have appeared on our labels, plus many more. Featured are 100 fabulous, kitchen-tested recipes made with a variety of Campbell's condensed and ready-to-serve soups, with 55 dishes ready in 30 minutes or less! Inside you'll find easy-to-prepare one-dish casseroles, skillet dishes, stir-fries, soups, stews, and much more. Dozens of recipes are beautifully photographed in color. When you put the famous Campbell label on mealtime at your home, family and friends will flip for these versatile, delicious dishes.

Hardcover book: 8x8 inches, 96 pages, 51 color recipe photographs, 100 recipes. Price $6.50 each; includes postage and handling.

"How to Order"

Indicate books desired and enclose a check or money order payable to Campbell Soup Company (no cash).

Item	Quantity	U.S. Order	Canadian Order	Total
Pace 50th anniversary cookbook *Family Recipe Round-Up*		$9.95	$13.50	
Swanson Broth *Easy Low-Fat Recipes*		$6.50	$9.00	
Campbell's *Back Label Recipes and more!*		$6.50	$9.00	

Send orders to:

**Campbell's Cookbook Offer
P.O. Box 9267, Dept. P
St. Cloud, MN 56398-9267**

Name: _____
(please print)

Address: _____ Apt.#: _____

City: _____ State: _____

Phone: _____ Zip: _____

Please allow 8 weeks for handling. Offer good only in U.S.A., Canada, Puerto Rico, and U.S. military installations. Void if taxed, restricted or prohibited by law. An offer of Campbell Soup Company, Campbell Place, Camden, NJ 08103-1799. Offer valid until 12/31/97 or while supplies last.